# MODERN WORLD

## IDEAS AND IDEALS

VENKATA MOHAN

# Contents

# Preface

Why do we have a president and a prime minister, instead of having all power concentrated in one position? We know that we borrowed our political structure from the English, but why did they develop it that way? What is fascism? Did Lenin follow what Marx wrote? How is communism different from socialism? Why did the USSR break up?

This book traces the history of the modern world from the Reformation to the end of the Cold War, attempting to answer many such questions by explaining not just the historical events but the ideas and ideals that shaped them. This would also help you to have a better insight into modern Indian history and polity by placing them in a larger context.

Venkata Mohan

May 2022

# Also By Venkata Mohan

1. Political Thought
2. IR Theory
3. India Among Nations
4. Cultural Anthropology
5. Caste & Religion in India
6. Tribal India & Social Thought
7. Sociological Thought
8. Economy: Concepts & Issues
9. Anthropological Thought
10. Ethical Thought
11. Moksha, Afterlife & Science

# 1500-1900 AD

CHAPTER ONE

# The Reformation

The Reformation refers to the reform of Christianity in the early modern era, which led to dividing the Christians into Catholics and Protestants. The person responsible for the Reformation is Martin Luther (1483–1546). Martin Luther did not intend to split Christianity, he only wanted to reform it, but the split happened anyway. The Protestants came out as a new sect, with the Catholics constituting the main group. In the 16th century when it happened, the Reformation contributed to the process of modernisation.

## *1. Reformation as democracy*

How could religious reform contribute to the modernisation of society? Religion includes the notion of God, scriptures, and priests. In India there were the Brahmins, in Christianity too there were priests, whose head was the pope. In any religion, people are interpreting the scriptures in a particular way, acting as intermediaries between God and people.

That was how some humans were ruling over other humans in the name of God. The bishops were controlling the people, the pope was ruling over the people. There was a hierarchy of the clergy. Because it was related to God, this hierarchy had great control over the minds of the people. It was oppressive and dictated things in many important matters of this life and the afterlife. Heaven, hell, sin, good, bad – the priests imposed a particular moral code on the people.

What would defying this hierarchy mean? It would mean empowering people and contributing to democracy. How did this defiance happen? Some of the religious people started defying the Church's authority. It is easier to defy the priests, rather than the scriptures or the belief in God. It is very difficult to say that God does not exist, or that the prophet is wrong, or to say that 'I am the new prophet'. It is easier to say that priests are wrong though the scriptures are right.

The reformers said the Christian scriptures are more important and not the authorities like the pope. But they did not say that they would interpret them right and that others should follow it. They only said, use your reason to interpret the scriptures yourself. An individual was assumed to be capable of interpreting the scriptures without any help from any intermediaries.

One can have a direct relationship with God, just like in the Indian tradition of Bhakti. In medieval India, some people criticised Brahminism, they said the rituals were not needed and anyone can have a direct relationship with God through bhakti or personal devotion. That was the Bhakti Movement, in which many scriptures were also rejected in addition to the priests and rituals. In Christianity, the reformers said it is only faith (equivalent to bhakti) that is needed, and no intermediary is necessary. When they said, you can interpret the scriptures yourself, there need not be an intermediary between you and God, this gave importance to individuals. The importance is given to the hierarchy and the intermediaries were taken away. The emphasis was on a direct relationship with God. A rebellion against religious authority helped in laying the foundation of democracy.

On what basis could the reformers claim that the scriptures were being misinterpreted and only their interpretation was right? They said we are going by our conscience. This was similar to the stance Socrates took long ago. The Reformation thus contributed to conscience-based thinking. People should learn, they should think for themselves and go by their conscience. This was how the Reformation became a part of the process of democratisation.

## 2. The abuses by the Church

One of the very serious abuses involving the Church at that time was the sale of indulgences. An indulgence was a kind of certificate that absolved a particular sin of the person buying it. So you can freely commit any sin, buy an indulgence and get away with any sin. These indulgences were being sold by the pope using the entire clerical establishment.

In 1457, the pope announced that the indulgences that could be bought now could be applied even to the souls of the family members or friends suffering in purgatory. Purgatory refers to the halfway station between hell and heaven. If you want a family member or a friend to come quickly out of the purgatory, the realm of punishment, then you can buy an indulgence for them. It was said in this context, "The moment the money tinkles in the collecting box, a soul flies out of purgatory!"

The people were so gullible and the clergy became increasingly exploitative. Certainly, the concept of indulgence had no basis whatsoever on what Jesus might have said about sin. If you sinned, how could you simply buy forgiveness? This was a glaring abuse of the Church's authority.

Further, the Church offices themselves were being sold. Those who had the money were buying them. Many unqualified bishops were appointed. There was also widespread nepotism, with the posts being awarded to relatives. Many priests charged exorbitant fees for religious activities, including burials. And many of the priests were not seen to be following any morals. A fifth of priests was maintaining concubines while they were supposed to remain unmarried and chaste.

Since 1215, the faithful were required to confess at least once a year. Such a practice of confession was very important in Christianity though it does not exist in religions like Hinduism. And if a person was not willing to confess, the priest would pressure him or her to make one. The practice of confession often became an interrogation by the priest.

The fact that such practices were there shows that the people were so ignorant. There was no literacy. There was no printing press. If a book was written, there would only be a few copies made, and very few people read those books. There was nothing like mass printing, nothing like mass education. Such a distorted form of Christianity was the official ideology for a long time. No wonder some scholars, even before Martin Luther, began to criticise the Church.

## *3. Early critics*

John Wycliffe (1328–84) was an English cleric and a scholar. He was against the Church accumulating wealth, he de-emphasised rituals. He said the scripture is the authority, not the Church. Unworthy popes need not be obeyed. Every man should interpret the scripture for himself.

Wycliffe also rejected transubstantiation – the belief that during the Mass the priest transforms ordinary bread and wine into the body and blood of Christ. In this ritual, the priest becomes very important. Wycliffe said that transubstantiation is not true, ordinary bread and wine cannot be equated with the body and blood of Christ. Even now some Catholics believe in this idea, it is a regular practice in a Catholic church, but Wycliffe rejected it so many centuries ago. Also, he got the Bible translated from Latin into English.

Jan Hus (1369–1415) was a Czech reformer, who was influenced by John Wycliffe. He considered the popes to be "anti-Christs." Unlike Wycliffe though, Hus was subjected to a gruelling death. In 1414, he was asked to attend the Council of Constance which was called to discuss reform. He was arrested there and put on trial for heresy. The Council condemned him and turned him over to the Holy Roman emperor, who ordered him to be burnt at the stake as a heretic.

Jan Hus

In those days, the people who were considered heretics by the Church were burnt at the stake. Because Hus criticised the abuses of the Church and because of his other teachings, he was considered a heretic. Hus said that the bishops were trying to be rich and powerful, seeking power rather than religion. He said all people are equal before God. All kinds of people, great and small, including prostitutes, came to listen to him. He said it is only repentance that leads to forgiveness and not any certificate issued by any man. “There is only you and God” – no one in between. He became a martyr, and his followers came to be called Hussites.

These developments took place before Martin Luther. This shows that Protestantism had deeper roots. By the time of Martin Luther, things were ripe for Protestantism to happen. Such was the Europe of the 16th century where there were discussions about whether there should be any intermediaries between God and man. Europe had been that at that time. Christianity had been that at that time. This shows how rapid modernization was.

## *4. Martin Luther*

Martin Luther

Martin Luther, a cleric, studied philosophy and law before becoming a monk. He went on to become a professor of theology. He then became a critic of the Church. The Bible talks about many sins and Jesus said, if you have a bad thought, that thought is equivalent to sinful action. If you commit adultery in thought, that is as bad as committing actual adultery. Jesus is very particular about thought processes – at least some people took Bible that way.

Martin Luther was a very serious monk and he wanted to cleanse his mind. He did all kinds of things, but no matter what he tried he could not get rid of the so-called impure thoughts.

Martin Luther said, "I was trying to cure the doubts and scruples of the conscience with human remedies. The more I tried these remedies, the more troubled and uneasy my conscience grew." He was not able to purify his mind. I think this is a simple process, if you try not to have any sexual thoughts, for example, you will get so many. And if you try to suppress envious thoughts, you will get so many of them too.

Martin Luther did not want such thoughts. He concluded that purifying the mind is not possible, but would that mean that everybody has evil thoughts and we are all condemned to go to hell? Martin Luther thought it cannot be so, there has to be a solution. He thought, you cannot avoid sin through your effort, but then how can it be avoided? He then realised that sin can be avoided only through faith.

Martin Luther concluded that the Bible itself offered the solution to this problem. "The just shall live by faith" (Romans 1:17). The just shall live by faith and faith alone. He then thought that if it is *only* faith that can make you free from sin, and your actions cannot help you, then what is the pope doing, what are the bishops doing? They were giving the impression that if you did something, you could be free from sin. He, therefore, started criticising the entire role of the pope. Luther's objections rose from a spiritual basis, not from a political basis. He was convinced that the pope was wrong and he chose to make his criticism public.

Martin Luther posted his criticism on the church door at Wittenberg, where he was working, on October 31, 1517. It was called the Ninety-Five Theses. What he wrote was distributed as pamphlets in vernacular German and very soon it became popular. In 1520, Pope Leo X excommunicated Martin Luther. Later, he was also made an outlaw by Holy Roman Emperor Charles V who also the king of Britain. This meant anybody could kill Martin Luther and the murderer wouldn't be punished. Martin Luther was no longer under the protection of a state.

But Martin Luther got protection from Frederick III, the ruler of Saxony. After the judgement of excommunication, Luther was taken to some secret location by Frederick III. There was a huge difference between how Jan Hus was treated and how Martin Luther was treated. Jan Hus was burnt alive, but Martin Luther was only excommunicated and he could find different patronage. This was because Martin Luther was popular and many people by then were convinced of his arguments and the unholy things that the Church was doing.

Luther's defiance of the emperor is inspiring. In a meeting where he was asked to retract, he refused to do so, saying to the emperor, "I am bound by the Scripture I have quoted and my conscience is captive to the word of God. I cannot and will not retract anything, since it is neither safe or right to go against conscience."

Luther was not simply criticising the pope, he would preach the beauty of Jesus' teachings, asking people to be compassionate and do great things. He talked about what life should be. He gave many discourses. People felt that this was the real teaching of Jesus, and it had nothing to do with the things that the pope and the bishops were doing.

There took place important political development at this time. The pope acted from Rome, the Church wielded its authority from Rome, and Martin Luther belonged to Germany. The German rulers did not like the pope's authority. Those were the days of growing nationalism. Many rulers in Europe were not happy with what the pope and the entire religious establishment was doing.

Indulgences were taking away the money from people, that would have gone towards taxes otherwise. Pope was controlling many other things. This was a conflict between the rulers and the religious establishment. Luther, a cleric, defying the pope was convenient for many rulers. Many people were also convinced by this time that the Church committed a grave atrocity in killing Jan Hus. Martin Luther himself was equated with Jan Hus. Thus, nationalism and anti-Church feelings made Martin Luther more popular. By this time the printing press was also being widely used. Many people could read.

Interestingly, because Martin Luther believed that one cannot go to heaven simply through one's actions, he rejected the monastic life also. He thought people can marry. He married too. In a way, he rejected the demands of poverty and chastity as being important for religious life.

Luther may have come to criticise the Church through a certain process of reasoning, but that was not so important to the people who could understand his criticism of the Church in their way. It was the fact that he was willing to risk his life for his convictions that made him a champion of a great cause. Luther's idea that good works and good thoughts do not take a person to heaven can make a great part of any religion irrelevant – but Protestantism started flourishing through the sheer emphasis on faith.

## *5. Jean Calvin*

Jean Calvin

Jean Calvin (1509–64), a French lawyer, made the Protestant movement an international rebellion. He was exiled to Switzerland because of his Protestantism. Luther saw himself as German, but Calvin had a universal outlook. In his book The Institutes of the Christian Religion (1536), Calvin posited a radical theory of foreordination: "For all are not created in equal conditions; rather, eternal life is foreordained for some, eternal damnation for others." This is also called the theory of predestination.

Luther said it is faith alone that will take you to heaven and not your actions, but Calvin went even further and said that even faith doesn't make any difference, whether you are going to heaven or hell is already predetermined. But what is common to both these views is that your actions would not make any difference to your afterlife.

Calvin said that if it is already decided that you are going to heaven, then you are likely to behave in a particular way. You will lead a "sober living," it is a sign of election by God. You will lead a simple life but you will work hard. Calvinists came to think if you are predestined to go to heaven, you will work, earn money but will lead a life of an ascetic. You will invest your money and make further money. Much later, in the late 19$^{th}$ century, this view of life came to be called the "Protestant Ethic."

According to Max Weber, it was this Protestant Ethic (which he called 'this worldly asceticism', in contrast to the otherworldly asceticism of monks) that gave rise to capitalism. Till then the Christian religion condemned money-lending for profit. But Calvin distinguished between usury and productive loans. He said one can give loans for productive purposes, at less interest rate. These things contributed to capitalism.

More than Lutherans, Calvinists treated lay and clerical people alike as equal members. There was no hierarchy of clerics. Whereas Lutheranism was confined to Germany, Calvinism spread to many parts of Europe, by 1570.

Was Weber right in concluding that Calvinism led to capitalism? It was more likely for things to be the other way around. Capitalism was emerging independently, commerce was growing independently and because of these economic developments the Christian religion developed in a particular way. That is how I see it, I do not think capitalism with its pursuit of greed is in tune with the teaching of Jesus. The Protestant ethic came to be what it was because the economy shaped it so. To Weber, the Protestant ethic shaping economy disproves Marx's idea that economy shapes religion, but Weber does not seem right in his conclusions to me.

## *6. Counter Reformation*

The Church's response to Reformation is called the Catholic Reformation or Counter Reformation. Many cases of abuse of the Church were stopped, indulgences were stopped. This was a huge change. Moral values came to be emphasised. The Catholic Reformation also encouraged individual forms of devotion and spirituality.

The history of the Western countries in the centuries that followed the Reformation was about the conflict between Catholics and Protestants. The sectarian conflict divided people within nations and contributed to the conflict between nations.

Some popes tried to reform the Church. Pope Paul III (serving between 1534–49) made such an attempt. Pius V (1566–72) declared war on venality and luxury. But some popes wanted to contain criticism rather than reform. Pope Paul IV (1555–59) created an index of forbidden books to ensure that Catholics would not read what was critical of the teaching of the Church.

In 1540, the Society of Jesus, or the Jesuits, was formed by St. Loyola to win back the Protestants. This effort had the support of the pope. The Jesuit order succeeded in winning back some Protestants and converting many other people to Catholicism across the world.

The sectarian conflict in Christianity led to higher literacy and the spread of mass education. The Protestants started educating the people at first, and later the Catholic Church too started saying that people should know what the scripture was, the priests themselves should know. The biblical teachings became more popular as more and more people could read and know what the scripture was saying.

An important legacy of the Reformation was the inculcation of the spirit of rationality among the people. When you start thinking and questioning matters of religion, nothing stops you from doing so in other areas as well. Europe became what it was not because it had a superior religion but because it questioned its religion. The Reformation is part of the Age of Enlightenment, which is what made Europe what it is.

The concept of secularism as the proper relationship between the state and religion, evolved in Europe, in the context of the conflict between Protestants and Catholics. This thinking evolved in Europe and later spread to many other countries.

## *Think on it*

1. What is the Reformation?
2. What is a sect?
3. Did the Christian reformers question scriptures?
4. How was the Reformation a part of the process of democratisation?
5. What were the abuses practised by the Church before the Reformation?
6. Who were the critics of the Church before the Reformation?
7. How did Martin Luther conclude that one can't go to heaven through one's efforts?
8. Why was Martin Luther outlawed?
9. What contributed to the popularity of Martin Luther's ideas?
10. What is the Protestant ethic?
11. How did the Protestant ethic contribute to the rise of capitalism, according to Weber?
12. What was Counter Reformation?

13. Why is the Reformation a part of the Age of Enlightenment?
14. What is secularism in the context of Europe?

CHAPTER TWO

# The English Revolution

The political arrangements in modern democratic society came into existence from the English Revolution. In India, we have a president, a prime minister, Lok Sabha, Rajya Sabha, the Supreme Court, and there is a separation of powers between legislature, executive and judiciary. How did this system come about? It did not come about as a result of conscious deliberation among some people. It simply evolved from a previously existing system, going through incremental changes over time. This evolution originally took place in England, and we based our Indian system on the English model. The parliamentary form of government developed over centuries in England and finally fell into place in 1689 with what is called the English Revolution or the Glorious Revolution.

## *1. Evolution of parliamentary system*

This was the traditional arrangement in a monarchy: You had a king and there were some advisers, the advisers were merely advisers and the king had all the powers. In the modern system, we have a president and a prime minister, and the prime minister has the real power though technically he is an advisor. How did this change happen, how did the legislature come to acquire power?

The story starts with the Magna Carta in England, in 1215 CE. The landowners were being heavily taxed and if they did not pay the taxes, they were imprisoned. There was a revolt of the landowners against the king. The tenants-in-chief secured the

Magna Carta, meaning the "Great Charter," from King John (r. 1199–1216) – which established that the king may not collect any new taxes without the consent of a "great council" that represented the barons, as the landowners were called. The council was no longer a purely advisory body, it had powers. This council turned into a parliament when King Edward I (r. 1272–1307) summoned the bishops and representatives from major towns, along with the barons, to seek funds. The parleys (meaning 'consultations') among these people came to be known as parliament.

During the reign of Edward III (r. 1327–77) the parliament got divided into two, the elected part and the nominated part. The House of Commons consisted of landowners and other representatives of towns, while the House of Lords consisted of nobles nominated by the monarch. For a long time, the parleys had been only on matters of taxation, but as taxation became more important with the king requiring more funds, the role of the parliament too became more important.

How did the system of a prime minister and his cabinet come about? The king used to send his trusted friends to mediate with the parliament. Later the House of Commons came to have a say over whom the king could send on his behalf to the parliament. Then came the party system. When this happened, the king's advisers belonged only to the party in power, and the leader of these advisers became the prime minister.

Thus, the parliamentary system evolved in England and was adopted in other places. This is why we have a nominal head, a real head, and two houses of the legislature.

## *2. Execution of Charles I*

Charles I

Some very important developments took place during the rule of Charles I (r. 1625–49). After the death of Queen Elizabeth in 1603, James I (r. 1603–25) became the king. Defending royalty, James I said, "Kings are not only God's lieutenants upon earth and sit upon the throne, but even by God himself they are called gods." James I thought he had the divine right to rule and this alienated the parliament.

James I was succeeded by his son Charles I who was as difficult as his father. The landowners were forced to give loans to the king, without the consent of the parliament. The king imprisoned those who did not give the loans. When the parliament began to object strongly, Charles I dissolved it in 1629.

When the Scots rose in revolt on the issue of governance of the Church of Scotland, Charles needed money to raise an army to fight against them. The parliament was summoned in 1640 for that purpose, but it refused to cooperate. They felt that the king was autocratic and if he raised a new army, it could be used against them. Then the king decided that he would raise a new army without the parliament's consent. The parliament did not like it and chose to raise its army against the king, something that never happened before.

The clash between these two armies led to a civil war in 1642. Religion played a central role in this war. The parliament was led by Puritans, who were a group of Calvinists that had emerged during Elizabeth's reign. These Calvinists were radical thinkers in many ways, they advocated a personal understanding of the Bible and devotion to God, they held simplicity and disciplined life as their ideals. Around 10% of England's population was composed of these Puritans.

As the civil war continued, Oliver Cromwell (1599–1658) who was a devoted Puritan with strong religious convictions emerged as a leader. In Calvinism, an 'elect' means a person chosen by God to go to heaven, and Cromwell thought he was an elect. Cromwell developed a new army in 1645 and called it New Model Army. He chose people who were disciplined, willing to obey him, and who believed in the cause of their fight. He also placed many commoners in leadership positions. Protestantism believed in empowering the common people, it was a new sect with a new ideology. The Protestants had a strong conviction that they were right. To Cromwell and his followers, the war was a religious war, what we would call jihad in Islamic terminology.

Charles I was defeated and apprehended in 1647, but he managed to escape. He was then brought back and the army thought much about what to do with him. Meanwhile, Cromwell did not want to become the king, as the people now had a new ideology that there should not be a king. They were trying to figure out what could be an alternative to a king.

Cromwell was unsure of what to do with Charles I and then concluded that the king should be killed. However, not everyone in the parliament was convinced about it.

By not allowing some inconvenient members to allow the session, the army ensured that the rump parliament passed a resolution that the king should be tried. The king was quickly found guilty and was executed on Jan 30, 1649. Charles I became the first monarch in world history to be tried and executed by his own people. Thus one thousand years of monarchy in England came to an end. But the people did this without having any idea of an alternative.

## *3. Cromwell's rule*

Oliver Cromwell

Cromwell couldn't call himself a king, but there had to be a leader, so he called himself Lord Protector and ruled England from 1653 to 1658. And he ruled with unlimited power. He imposed taxes without parliamentary approval and purged the parliament in 1653. In its place, he picked up 140 people whom he regarded as saints. But he was not happy with this new parliament too and it too was dissolved after six months.

Cromwell imposed many taxes on the people because he waged many wars. He defeated the Irish and the Scots. He also went to war with the Dutch and Spain. He gave religious freedom to all Puritan sects but not to Catholics. He thus turned out to be a more despotic ruler than a king would normally be. In 1657, a newly elected parliament offered him the position of king, but he refused. Because many people in the army felt that they fought the war not to make somebody a king again, Cromwell thought he would lose the support of the army if he declared himself the king. He continued to rule nevertheless. He re-introduced the second house of Parliament, whose members would be appointed by him. He also claimed the right to name his successor just as any king would.

After Cromwell's death, he was succeeded by his less able son, Richard, after whom many successors ruled ineffectively. Then the people thought this system was of no use and felt they should restore kingship.

## *4. The Levellers*

Many radical ideas were being discussed in England around that time. In Cromwell's New Model Army, there was a radical group called Levellers, which wanted new laws that would protect the poor as well as the rich. They wanted a broader electoral franchise, though the property was still a criterion as "a permanent fixed interest in this kingdom" was needed. But there was another group in the army who called themselves Diggers. They opposed all private ownership of land. They considered themselves to be true Levellers. Some of these Leveller regiments even participated in a mutiny though they were crushed.

The London Levellers wrote in what was called the Agreement of the People "The poorest man in England is not at all bound in a strict sense to that government that he has not had a voice to put himself under." That's to say, if the common man is not given a chance to express himself, then he is not to be subjected to the government.

Cromwell was not at all interested in such radical ideas. But the issues the Levellers raised have historical importance. They were talking about socialism and universal adult franchise though they did not use those words. The Levellers played an important role in the decision to eliminate the king, they were also the main reason why Cromwell did not accept the position of a king.

## 5. *Restoration of monarchy*

The parliament negotiated with the exiled son of Charles I and he was asked to be the new king. Charles II ruled England from 1660 to 1685. He disbanded the New Model Army and wanted to revenge on his father's execution. He got Cromwell's body dug up and hung on the 12$^{th}$ anniversary of the execution of Charles I.

Charles II appointed his trusted friends to answer parliamentary questioning. He favoured the ministers who were Catholic. He signed a secret treaty with Louis XIV, the French monarch, that he would eventually restore Catholicism in England. He also tried to change certain laws affecting Catholics. The parliament was Protestant, the Church was Protestant, but the king wanted to bring back Catholicism to England and this alienated many people.

It was in this context that two factions emerged in the parliament, those who espoused parliamentary supremacy, called Whigs, and those who supported the divine-right monarchy, called Tories. The opposition from parliament to King Charles II became intense. In 1681, he attempted to rule without the parliament and got some Whigs executed on the charge of plotting to kill him.

## 6. *Glorious Revolution*

Charles II was succeeded by his brother James II, who also began to dismiss advisers who were not Catholics. He too tried to restore Catholicism as the state religion in England. But the people thought that his Catholicism would die with him as he did not have any male heirs. It so happened that when the queen was pregnant, James II predicted the birth of a son and a Catholic heir to the throne. It meant Catholicism would not end with him. It even sparked the rumours that the new-born was not really the king's son but a surrogate baby.

The parliament wanted to get rid of the king and his Catholicism. One of James II's daughters by a previous marriage, Mary, had married a Protestant Dutchman, William of Orange. A group of parliamentarians asked William to invade England.

William landed in England with 15,000 men, and James II fled to France. The parliament invited William and Mary to occupy a double throne. It was this act that came to be known as the Glorious Revolution of 1689. There was no violence or bloodshed, there was nothing like a great event – so why was it called a revolution and also a glorious one? This simple act of the parliament set a template for the future working of the political system. The parliament made two people king and queen and determined their role in a system in which they could not step beyond its authority.

The issue at the surface level was between Catholicism vs Protestantism, but at a deeper level, it was an issue of king vs people. The clarity regarding the political arrangements that was absent among the people at the time of the execution of Charles I came by the time of the Glorious Revolution.

Then the parliament passed a Bill of Rights, which signified the shift of sovereignty to the people as represented by their parliament. From this time, the laws were to be made only by the parliament and the king could not suspend them by himself. Earlier it was only about the taxation powers, but now any law could only be made by the parliament and the king would not be able to suspend them. Further, the judiciary was to be independent of royal pressures. The freedom of worship was extended to all Protestants, including non-Anglican Protestants. It said that the throne should always be held by a Protestant because Protestantism was the religion of the people. And the king had to be of the same religion as the people.

All this meant that the sovereignty now lay with the people and not with the king. The Bill of Rights is considered a landmark document in the evolution of constitutional governments.

## *7. Limited government*

Around this time, the political philosopher John Locke (1632–1704) developed some clear ideas about a democratic government. He was a friend of some of the landowners who sent James II into exile. Locke argued that the rights of individuals and their property rights should be protected. He also advocated religious toleration. It was Locke's framework that was followed in the creation of a constitutional monarchy in England.

In the context of England, the fight was between the king and the parliament, the parliament being the representative of the people. But Locke's theory is not simply about the rights of the parliament. He argued that the purpose of the government itself is that it cannot take away certain rights of the people. The government includes the parliament.

At the time of Magna Carta, it started as a fight for the rights of the landowners, and by the time of the Glorious Revolution, it became a fight for all the basic rights of the people against any violation by the government, including the king, the parliament and the judiciary. This was the concept of limited government that John Locke advocated. These basic rights came to be called "inalienable" rights, also known as fundamental rights in the Indian context. The upholding of these rights protects people and society from the encroachment of the state.

## *Think on it*

1. What are the basic elements of a parliamentary system?
2. What do you know about the Magna Carta?
3. How did the cabinet system evolve in England?
4. Why did the British parliament raise its own army?
5. How did Oliver Cromwell do as a military commander?
6. Why was Charles I beheaded?
7. How did Oliver Cromwell rule England as its Lord Protector?

8. What do you know about the Levellers?
9. Why was kingship restored in England?
10. What was glorious about the Glorious Revolution?
11. What is Bill of Rights?
12. What is the concept of limited government?

CHAPTER THREE

# The American Revolution

The American Revolution was an independence movement – independence from British rule. It can be seen as a part of the trend of decolonisation. We can understand the American independence movement better when we contrast it with our independence movement in India because they were so different.

## *1. Independence in the Americas*

What independence meant to us in India was the same as what it meant to most Asian and African countries, but independence in the American context was different.

The north and south American continents were together called the New World. The Europeans discovered it in the 15$^{th}$ century, and when they landed there, they found that there were people there already. How did those people get there before Columbus and others first set foot in this New World?

The New World is separated from the rest of the world by a huge stretch of ocean, but these natives got there thousands of years ago through migration from Siberia to Alaska. When we see the world map, we see Siberia on one side and Alaska on the other side, so we get the impression that they are too distant from each other, being on two different sides. But as we can see on a globe, they are not on two different sides, they are very close to each other and many thousands of years ago they were connected by a land bridge.

The human race migrated from Africa to Europe and Asia, and then many people moved north to Siberia, from where they entered Alaska. All the people living on all the continents today are the descendants of those humans who moved out from Africa, over 65,000 years ago. This is called the "Out of Africa" theory. When the Europeans discovered America, it was a clash of two civilisations – the Europeans were far more advanced than the natives, who were also called Indians. Columbus was trying to reach India when he found that land, he thought he reached India and so he called the people there Indians.

The conflict between the Europeans and the natives was very violent, many of the natives were killed and their lands were taken away. Eventually, a few European countries occupied the entire New World.

Independence in America or the other countries of the New World was not for the natives from the Europeans. Independence in America meant independence for the people of the European stock living in America for a few generations – from the European governments. It was the same in the countries of South America as well. The people of European origin living in those countries cut off their ties with the governments of the European countries. In the case of America, many British people arrived and settled there, and the so-called American Revolution was the independence of these colonies from the British mainland.

The upper classes in American colonies were pitted against the upper classes in England. This was a different scene from that in India over a century later: the colonial masters educating the natives, leaders emerging from the natives and getting the colonial rulers out. In America, it was a fight between two groups of people belonging to the same advanced civilisation. Modern ideas played an important role at a very early stage in the struggle. Only some small events triggered their fight for independence.

What was the main triggering point? Britain imposed certain taxes on the American people which they did not like. Britain had been involved in two wars with France and the natives, it was in huge losses, and so it thought to extract some money from the Americans. But the Americans would not tolerate it.

There was also another issue about the American colonies not being represented in the British parliament – because of which companies in Britain gained an advantage over business classes in America in doing business in America. The British parliament did certain things which were favourable to English companies, and this was affecting the American merchants. It was a commercial clash.

These two issues gave rise to the demand for no taxation without representation. The British could have given representation for the Americans in the British parliament, but the king called the American demand a rebellion. Then the war between the British army and the army of the colonists, which was called the Continental Army, ensued and the colonies became independent states at the end of it.

## *2. The events*

Before the American Revolution, Britain was involved in two wars. One of them was the Seven Years War with France that took place between 1756 and 63. There was also another war with the natives in America. The British won these two wars, but at a great cost. They wanted to recuperate the losses and impose taxes on the colonies. In March 1765, the Stamp Act was passed in the British parliament. It required many documents printed in America only on paper stamped in Britain.

This development resulted in mounting tensions between England and America. Five years later, in 1770, there was an event called the Boston Massacre. When you hear this word 'massacre', you would think that some great atrocity happened, with hundreds of people dying. Do you know how many people died? In all, five people and the Americans called it a massacre. The pictures of this event show British troops firing on unarmed crowds, but it can give one a wrong idea, such pictures are misleading.

What happened was, on March 5, 1770, an altercation arose between a British soldier and an American citizen, a Bostonian, and some other Bostonians joined the fray. The soldier felt threatened. To defend him, seven other soldiers moved in. Then about two hundred Bostonians came to the spot. In that scuffle, the soldiers fired at the people, which resulted in 5 deaths.

It was not that a peaceful protest was happening and the soldiers came and opened fire. Interestingly, though this event was used as propaganda by the revolutionaries, John Adams, who would become the second president of America (1797–1801), defended the soldiers on the ground that what they did was in self defence.

The Boston Massacre took place as there had been growing tensions between the British and the Americans at that time. Two years earlier, on June 10, 1768, the British customs officials in Boston seized an American sailboat, Liberty, for alleged smuggling and confiscated it. The subsequent events led to rioting due to which customs officials fled. This led to the British army being stationed there.

The next important event was the Boston Tea Party which took place on December 16, 1773. A group of men led by Samuel Adams, disguising themselves as Native Americans, boarded a ship carrying tea and dumped all the 342 chests of tea into the sea. This incident took place particularly as a reaction to the Tea Act that was passed by the British parliament some months ago to help the British East India Company. The Act allowed the company to sell tea in America without having to pay taxes except for the import duty under the Townshend Acts which were created to raise revenue from the colonies. At that time, more than 80% of tea consumed in America was smuggled Dutch tea.

The American merchants did not like the favour given to a British company. The American protestors could prevent tea from Britain unloading at the other ports but they couldn't do that in Boston. The British official at Boston refused to send the ship back to Britain. So the protesters boarded the ship and dumped the tea. Why did they disguise as native Americans? It was partly to hide their identity and partly to say that they identified with America and not with Britain. The British were shocked by this act, and in reaction, the British parliament passed many punitive acts, what are called the Intolerable Acts in America. What were these Acts?

The Boston Port Act said the Boston port would be closed until the colonists paid for the cost of the destroyed tea, which amounted to around one million dollars in today's money. The next one was the Massachusetts Government Act. Boston came under the Massachusetts government. This Act said that town meetings, where people took important decisions, were not allowed without the governor's approval. This meant restricting Americans' right to self-government.

The third one was the Administration of Justice Act, which said that any accused British officials would be tried back in Great Britain and not on American soil. A trial in Britain would be much more lenient compared to one on American soil before the American citizens.

The next one was the Quartering Act, which allowed a governor to house soldiers in unoccupied houses and buildings at any place. This would help Britain in stationing troops in many towns.

Britain passed these laws to put down the growing American resistance. But they only antagonised the Americans further. The colonists decided to come together and fight against the British. Then 56 delegates from the 13 colonies, except New York, met in October 1774, in Philadelphia. In this meeting, called the First Continental Congress, it was decided that the colonists would boycott all British goods.

## *3. The war*

The Americans petitioned King George to repeal the Intolerable Acts. But the king was not willing, nor did the British parliament think it was doing anything excessive against the Americans. This led to a war between the American colonies and Britain. It began in April 1775, about two years after the Boston Tea Party.

The colonists overthrew the existing governments in the 13 colonies, closed the courts and drove away the British officials. The American soldiers were local and more committed, while the British were less committed. There was not much commitment from the British parliament either to fight the Americans, with some of the members sympathising with the American cause.

On July 4, 1776, the Second Continental Congress in Philadelphia adopted the Declaration of Independence. In 1778, France joined the American side, France being a rival of Britain.

The war ended in October 1781. The Treaty of Paris was signed in 1783 and it recognised the 13 former colonies as sovereign states. All these colonies came together to form one country. For the first time, a major country became a republic. A republic is a form of government where the ruler is elected. Although Switzerland became a republic before the US, it was too small a country.

George Washington

The US constitution was framed in 1789. George Washington who was the commander-in-chief of the American army became the first president of the US and ruled from 1789 to 1797. George Washington had played a very important role in the American War of Independence, because of which he became hugely popular. He was unopposed as a presidential candidate.

## *4. Significance*

Some small events led to the war between Britain and America and eventually to American independence. The kind of political system that Americans wanted to create had a great influence on the world. The Declaration of Independence of 1776 was a monumental document. It was not a simple declaration of independence. They could have simply said, okay, we are forming a new state, now we are free from the British rule, we will favour our merchants, and we will rule ourselves. But that is not just what they said.

This Declaration of Independence was largely drafted by Thomas Jefferson, who became the third president of America (1801–1809). It had radical statements: "We hold these truths to be self-evident, that all men are created equal, that they are endowed by their Creator with certain unalienable rights, that among these are life, liberty, and the pursuit of happiness."

Nobody said this before with such clarity: All men are created equal. It was a grand statement though at that time they did not think of women, black slaves and natives as equals.

The Declaration said, "That, to secure these rights, governments are instituted among men, deriving their just powers from the consent of the governed." The government exists based on the consent of the governed, and the consent happens only upon the assurance of the protection of the rights of the people. This social contract argument was inspired by Locke and by the English Revolution.

Then the document says, "That, whenever any form of government becomes destructive of these ends, it is the right of the people to alter or to abolish it, and to institute new government, laying its foundation on such principles, and organizing its powers in such form, as to them shall seem most likely to effect their safety and happiness." This is a call for rebellion whenever and wherever governments become unjust.

Thomas Jefferson

The document puts forward grand ideals – not just for Americans, but for humankind. This is about justice and the right form of government. The Declaration is a promise that this new country is going to be different. It was radical in scope. The Glorious Revolution did not remove the king. The British couldn't have said that all men are created equal. The American Revolution was a huge leap from the concept of 'no taxation without representation ' to the notion that 'all men are created equal '.

These ideals are important. Over the decades and centuries that followed, whenever America was in crisis, the people looked up to these ideals and asked themselves: what are we to do now? About a hundred years later, Lincoln in his fight against slavery reaffirmed that all men are created equal. The implication of stating something as an ideal is that people strive to live by such an ideal and even if they fail at first to some extent or other, future generations can still do better in living up to it.

The American constitution was framed based on this Declaration of Independence. The constitution was adopted by Congress in 1789 and was ratified by most of the states by 1791. Ten amendments were added to the constitution when it came into effect. The First Amendment provides several rights to American citizens: the right to express ideas through speech or press, the right to assemble or gather with a group to protest or other reasons, and the right to ask the government to fix problems. It also protects the right to religious beliefs and practices. It prevents the government from favouring any particular religion. These ten amendments together are known as the Bill of Rights. They spell out Americans' rights concerning their government.

The American constitution amplified and clarified the democratic ideals which were not spelt out clearly in the English Revolution. The spirit of the American constitution inspired many revolutions in Latin America – a wave of revolutions that came to be known as the Atlantic Revolutions.

In the years that followed the American Revolution, there was some good progress in the direction of abolishing slavery. Slavery was abolished in the northern states by 1804. The southern states banned importing more slaves from Africa. The southern states also allowed the owners to free their slaves, but they still did not abolish slavery. Why this north-south difference regarding slavery? The economy of the southern states was based on slave labour, they had more to lose by abolishing slavery. The northern states were more industrialised and depended less on slavery.

Although the American Revolution was a turning point in humanity's struggle for democracy and freedom, the native Americans themselves did not get anything from it. Several natives were on the side of the British during the American War of Independence. Some natives were on the American side, but it did not matter. The natives had no role in the peace talks. Soon after

America expanded taking away many lands of the natives.

Despite some shortcomings, the American Revolution thus helped start a new era in the history of humanity. The ideals on which America founded itself turned out to be more impactful than any other political and economic ideals of any other revolution. To date, America seems to have got its fundamentals right, faring better than others in upholding democracy and freedom. The subsequent revolutions across the world turned out to be disasters – be it the French, the Russian or the Chinese.

## *Think on it*

1. Is the American Revolution an example of decolonisation?
2. How did people reach the Americas before the Europeans?
3. What is the 'Out of Africa' theory?
4. Why are the natives in the Americas called Indians?
5. What was the Boston Massacre? Why did it happen?
6. What was the Boston Tea Party? Why did it happen?
7. What were the Intolerable Acts?
8. What led to the American War of Independence?
9. What was the role of George Washington in the American Revolutionary War?
10. What are the goals of a state according to the Declaration of Independence?
11. Did the American Revolution provide equality to all Americans in practice?
12. What is the historical significance of the American Revolution?

CHAPTER FOUR

# The French Revolution

The French Revolution was different from the two revolutions preceding it. In the English and American revolutions, there were no major efforts at social change though they declared the equality of man. The French Revolution tried to change society, it tried to change politics, economy and religion. It was a comprehensive effort to change the entire social system. Something like the French Revolution had not been attempted before. But what was the outcome of it all?

Much violence took place during the years of the French Revolution. Some positive changes resulted but in the end, it led to the dictatorship of Napoleon. Many people asked why did it happen that way? Was the French Revolution a failure? And if so, why? What lessons can be drawn from the French Revolution?

Different people drew different lessons from it. Marx, Lenin and Mao thought the ideals of the French Revolution were not realised because of certain mistakes the leaders made. They felt that the ideals were worth realising and the mistakes can be avoided. But did the people behind the Russian and Chinese revolutions learn the right lessons or did they only end up repeating the mistakes of the French Revolution?

## *Great violence*

The French revolutionaries wanted to eliminate many people by inflicting minimum pain. They chose a newly-devised instrument for beheading people, called guillotine, but they might not have known that they would be killing tens of thousands of people with it. Between 11,000 to 18,000 people perished in the hands of the Committee on Public Safety, under the guillotine blade. About 300,000 people were imprisoned for at least some period during the years of this revolution. The revolution started as a rebellion of the poor against the rich, but over the years the violence grew and even many poor people were killed. Many of the revolutionaries themselves were killed by the guillotine.

Only about 15% of those killed were nobles or clergy, who constituted 5-8% of the population. The nobles were the aristocratic elite who had lands and privileged offices, and the clergy were the priests. Though a higher proportion of the upper classes were killed, 85% of those killed belonged to the lower classes.

This revolution was not only about the king vs the people, or the rich vs the poor, it was much more ambitious in its scope. The famous slogan of the French Revolution, which reflected its ideals, was: Liberty, Equality and Fraternity.

## *How it began*

The French king at that time was Louis XVI. And the people were not happy with their king. In the simplest kind of revolution, the absolute monarch would be replaced by a constitutional monarch. Forming a republic instead of a constitutional monarchy would be the next level of change, as in the American Revolution. But if we want a republic and also a considerable degree of social change, then that would be more difficult to realize.

At first, the French revolutionaries didn't think of any sweeping social changes. They wanted only to get a constitutional monarch, as in England. Alternatives to monarchy had been tried in England, but they failed. America could make a republic happen because there had been no monarchy there.

Had the king and the queen of France been intelligent and responded to the situation properly, there could have been a smoother transition to a constitutional monarchy along with more gradual changes in the society, and a lot of violence could have been avoided. But this was not the case.

When Louis XVI (1754–93) became the king in 1774, he was only 20 years old. This boy was not an able king and was not a good decision-maker. Earlier, the War of the Austrian Succession (1740 to 1747) and the Seven Years War (1756 to 1763) had weakened the country. Louis XVI was persuaded to give support to the American war, that too with money borrowed at high-interest rates. The king had to borrow at high-interest rates because the French financial system was ineffective without any central bank and he had to borrow from private parties. Further, there were poor harvests in 1787 and 1788. The financial situation in France was very bad. So new taxes had to be imposed. Taxes were the cause both for the English and the American revolutions.

The French society had three groups. Nobles and clergy were two important groups, they had much wealth but they were not paying any taxes. The others, the commoners, had to pay all the taxes. Louis XVI decided to summon what was called the Estates General, which was a parliament representing the three segments of the society, in connection with the proposal to raise the taxes. The last time it was convened was very long ago, in 1614. The Estates General consisted of three estates representing the three groups of people, and each estate had one vote. The first two estates made up only 3% of the population but held 40% real estate or land and even a higher share of income-producing enterprises.

As each estate had one vote, if the first and second estates united, they could dominate the third. The Third Estate, consisting of the commoners, did not like this situation. By now the Third Estate was represented by many lawyers who were influenced by the ideas of Enlightenment, the English Revolution and the American Revolution. They were also inspired by the ideas of the French thinkers Voltaire and Rousseau.

The Estates General of 1789 was convened at the Palace of Versailles, the royal residence, located some miles away from Paris.

There were a total of 1200 representatives, with half of them belonging to the Third Estate and the other half belonging to the first two estates. The Third Estate demanded a 'one man, one vote' approach. Based on 'one man, one vote,' the Third Estate would get a majority, given that it had sympathisers from the other estates too.

The First and Second Estates were not willing to give more voice to the Third Estate, and they were not willing to be taxed. The king was not in a position to rein in the first two estates. On June 20, 1789, when the representatives of the Third Estate arrived at the meeting, they found that the meeting hall was locked to them. Then they met in a nearby tennis court and decided to form a National Constituent Assembly. It was called the Tennis Court Meeting. The National Constituent Assembly was expected to frame a new constitution.

## *Storming of Bastille*

So far things were peaceful, but then there was a violent outbreak. July $14^{th}$, 1789 is considered the day when the French Revolution started. On this day a political prison and fortress known as Bastille was stormed because rumours spread that the National Assembly was going to be quashed. Thousands of people stormed the prison believing it was storing ammunition which they wanted to take hold of. The guards of the prison were killed. The severed head of the commander of the fortress was carried on a pike as a gesture of triumph through the streets of Paris. The National Assembly did not condemn this violence.

And after the fall of Bastille many rural revolts took place. Title deeds specifying obligations to the owners were burnt. In August 1789, the National Assembly formally abolished the feudal regime, it abolished personal labour servitude owed to the nobles. The king used to sell offices to get money, and that sale of offices was now abolished. The National Assembly also made the Church property national property. From now, the clergy had to swear allegiance to the nation. The entire religious establishment had to come under the government.

Then the National Assembly began drafting the constitution. They wanted to have a constitutional monarchy. The Assembly also promulgated the Declaration of Rights of Man and Citizen. It contained these freedoms.

Article I – Human Beings are born and remain free and equal in rights.

Article II – The goal of any political association is the conservation of the natural and imprescriptible rights of man. These rights are liberty, property, safety and resistance against oppression.

(Notice the mention of property above.)

Article III – The principle of any sovereignty resides essentially in the Nation.

Article IV – Liberty consists of doing anything which does not harm others.

Article V – The law has the right to forbid only actions harmful to society.

Article VI – The law is the expression of the general will.

Article VII – No man can be accused, arrested or detained but in the cases determined by the law, and according to the forms which it has prescribed.

In this way, there are a total of 17 articles in the declaration.

On October 5, 1789, some 10,000 people consisting of mostly women, went to Versailles to convince the king to provide them bread. When they tried to force their way into the palace, the guards shot a man dead. Then the people rebelled, two guards were killed and their heads were stuck on pikes. The king and the queen were forcibly brought back to Paris. The site of the National Assembly also was shifted to Paris.

The king and the queen wanted to escape. Where did they want to escape to? To Austria, because the queen hailed from there. The queen, Marie Antoinette (1755–93), played a significant role in causing the French Revolution. Her extravagant spending enraged the hundreds of thousands of poor, hungry people. When she became the queen, she was just 19-year-old. The king and the queen were like kids. She was the daughter of the Austrian Queen Maria Theresa. Austria was then a hostile power to France. This marriage took place as a part of strengthening the relations between the two countries.

While she was coming to France, Marie Antoinette was asked at the border to leave everything that belonged to Austria. She had to enter France without carrying any of her belongings, including her pet dog. At the palace, she was seen as an Austrian, a hostile person. She didn't experience love or concern from anyone. It was a very unhappy marriage. In addition, the king had a sexual problem, the marriage was not consummated. They did not have children for 7 years.

The duty of the queen was to produce an heir, but she was unable to do it, through no fault of hers. And at the end of the seven years, some surgery had to be done on the king and finally, they had offspring. But meanwhile, so much damage was done. The queen never went out of the palace. She did not know anything about politics. She was just all alone. And out of her unhappiness, she used to spend extravagantly. She was called Madame Déficit. Many illicit affairs too were attributed to her. She became an object of hatred for the whole nation.

And when the revolution started, the queen was guiding the king as he was indecisive. After they were taken to Paris, they planned to escape to Austria. In June 1791, the king and the queen tried to flee, but it was such a clumsily planned thing, they were also going with the whole royal fanfare and so they were easily caught and brought back. They were then accused of treason.

Till then, some people within the National Assembly were asking for a constitutional monarchy while others wanted to form a republic. But now there couldn't be any constitutional monarchy. The king was guillotined in January 1793, and the queen followed in the October of that year.

These developments also made France come into conflict with its neighbouring countries. Some people in the National Assembly wanted to start a war against Austria fearing it would invade. The war against Austria was declared in April 1792. Austria was joined by other countries including Prussia. But the French army was not ready for such a big confrontation. About 2/3rds of its officers deserted, as 85% of the officers had been nobles before the Revolution. The officers did not want the Revolution to succeed.

## *Radical changes in religion*

Some months after the revolution started, the people wanted to do something about the Church. As has been mentioned earlier, on Nov 2, 1789, the Church property, which constituted 10% of the nation's land, was confiscated and offered for sale. And next, on July 12, 1790, the Civil Constitution of the French Clergy was passed. The pope condemned it. Bishops could now make public pronouncements only with the authorisation of the government. The bishops were to be elected by the local assemblies.

In November 1790, the National Assembly proclaimed that all priests had to swear an oath of loyalty to the revolution. But between half to two-thirds of priests refused to take the oath. They were asked to take an oath saying that they were with the revolution. The people were divided in terms of their support to "non-juring" priests, those that were not willing to take the oath. And then some people refused to take sacraments from the "juring" clergy. The people were divided, the priests were divided, a counter revolution started.

If the counter revolution succeeds, the revolution would fail. And if the foreign powers succeed in the war, the revolution would fail. The counter revolution started in many areas of France. All these things caused more insecurity and uncertainty among the people. More and more people were being killed, not only in Paris but at other places too.

Who was seen to be on the side of the counter revolution? If someone was not being enthusiastic enough about the revolution, he was thought to be on the side of the counter revolution. If somebody was accused and if you said that it was unfair, that he didn't do anything – then you could be accused. You could be considered a collaborator. If somebody is accused, you would have to throw a stone at him just to save yourself. You might even provide some false evidence against him. This way everybody turned against everybody.

It seemed like the counter revolutionaries were everywhere. It seemed like the spies were everywhere. All this led to an atmosphere of fear. At the top political level, any disagreement could be a ground for an accusation against a leader of being a counter revolutionary.

In September 1792, during the wartime, some people went to the prison which was supposed to house many counter revolutionaries, and killed over 1200 people. This was called the September Massacre. Georges Danton (1759–1794), a lawyer, was responsible for inciting the September Massacre. He supported the foundation of the Revolutionary Tribunal, which was set up to try the counter revolutionaries and administer instant justice. He was the first president of the Committee of Public Safety. This was the committee that ordered thousands of deaths. But after 1793, Danton changed his mind on the use of force. When he started criticising the excesses of the committee, he was guillotined in 1794.

Maximilien Robespierre (1758–94), the most prominent revolutionary, was also guillotined in 1794. The leaders simply feared one another. So where is liberty in all this? Where is equality? Where is fraternity? It makes us wonder, how do people end up doing things this way? It also reminds us of what happened in the 20$^{th}$ century during the long and brutal regimes of Stalin and Mao.

Maximilien Robespierre

The counter revolution started in 1793. The National Convention was the assembly that governed France from September 1792 to October 1795. In 1793, the Convention framed a constitution to replace the constitution of 1791, and the rights of the people were much more limited now. On March 19, 1793, the Convention passed a law permitting the immediate trial of armed insurgents without a jury. The Committee of Public Safety that would be responsible for thousands of deaths was formed by the Convention, in 1793. It had twelve members. Maximillien Robespierre emerged as the committee's top leader. Under his leadership, terror became an important policy. He belonged to a group called Jacobians. Jacobians were some of the radical members of the National Convention, who used to meet in the house of the religious order of the Jacobians though they did not have anything to with their beliefs.

In September 1793, a campaign of de-Christianisation began. The churches were closed. The crosses on the altars were removed. Many among the clergy turned against the revolution because of this. In October 1793, a new calendar was instituted, and September 22, 1792, the birth date of the republic, became day 1 of the new calendar. Robespierre sought to establish a "Cult of Supreme Being." He wanted to create a "Republic of Virtue". In June 1794, the republic celebrated the "Festival of Reason." A cathedral was turned into "a temple of reason."

## *What went wrong?*

Edmund Burke, a British political thinker, predicted the failure of the French Revolution. He said, if you want to change something, keep something static as its basis. You stand on the static thing and try to change the other things. The problem with the French Revolution was that they were trying to change everything at once. The earlier order was a source of stability, but the French revolutionaries were trying to change everything at the same time. That was not going to work – so thought Burke.

I believe this revolution was conceptually flawed. Rousseau glorified society and undermined the individual. He identified inequality as the source of all problems. What caused the problem in this revolution was that society became far more important than the individual.

It is wrong to think that we can do anything to the individual to create an ideal society. The revolutionaries thought that they can also kill anybody to create a better society. Another wrong idea is that a good individual is only he who contributes to social ideals. So if you are not sufficiently enthusiastic about the revolution, then you are considered anti-society. If you disagree with the way it is going, then you are considered anti-society.

People started accusing each other. "You are selfish" – that is a serious charge. But why shouldn't a man be selfish? "You take care of yourself and not of the society" – that is a serious charge.

"You enjoy life" – another charge, or "You are not sufficiently enthusiastic about the revolution." All this is the complete opposite of liberty.

These revolutionaries refused to admit that they could be selfish. They refused to admit that individually they might be seeking power. They refused to admit that that is simply human nature. They refused to acknowledge that individual rights are important. The individual was not protected from society.

I think the latter-day revolutionaries, be it, Marx, Lenin or Mao, did not learn any lessons from the French Revolution and its failure. Because in the models Lenin and Mao tried, they too did not try to protect the individual. They only tried to crush the individuals to achieve the ideals of liberty, equality and fraternity – without seeing that liberty means the liberty of an individual, not of the society. When there is no individuality, there can be no fraternity. And equality without liberty and fraternity is meaningless.

Look at the things the French revolutionaries tried to do with religion. They wanted to de-Christianise the society. They did not see the depth of Christianity or the source of religion and spirituality. They did not realise the power of forgiving, as opposed to revenge. Going by them, even God should be elected!

They did not look at themselves, their urge for power, their fear, what kind of meaningless things they were doing to their friends and what kind of terror they were creating. It was just madness. They wanted to create the Republic of Virtue, they ended up creating the Republic of Vice.

If people had learnt the right lessons from the French Revolution, the Russian and Chinese revolutions would not have happened. The French Revolution showed how leaders could turn out to be monsters in the end. And when these revolutionaries were being killed publicly, the people were cheering.

I'd say, respect the individual. Respect individual liberty. Do not try to change people through violence. Only Locke understood liberty in the right sense, Rousseau did not. A revolution based on Rousseau's ideals wreaked havoc upon the whole country.

## *Think on it*

1. What do you know about the scale of violence during the French Revolution?
2. Why was the guillotine devised?
3. What was the financial situation of France before the Revolution?
4. When was the Estates General convened? What was the conflict among the estates?
5. When was the Bastille prison stormed? What was its significance?
6. What does the Declaration of Rights of Man and Citizen say?
7. Why were the king and queen guillotined?
8. Why did France have to go to war during the revolution?
9. What changes were brought in the religious establishment of France during the revolution?
10. What factors contributed to the counter revolution?
11. What do you know about Maximillien Robespierre?
12. What is the Reign of Terror?
13. How do you explain the failure of the French Revolution?

CHAPTER FIVE

# The Industrial Revolution

The Industrial Revolution transformed the world dramatically. It gave rise to capitalism and various political systems. The modern world is characterised and shaped by advances in technology that developed during the Industrial Revolution. The Industrial Revolution took place in the hundred years between 1750 and 1850, at first mainly in Britain till 1820, and then spread to France, Germany and other countries of northwestern Europe as well as to the United States.

The Industrial Revolution made mass production and mass consumption possible. The factory system emerged. Urbanisation happened on a bigger scale, and with it, some major cities arose. A greater degree of specialisation was taking place. The spread of industrialisation promoted colonialism and expanded its scope. The colonies became sources of raw materials. Great Britain and other European countries made finished products and were also using the colonies as additional markets for these products.

The Industrial Revolution also increased the connections between towns and cities by railways and telegraph. The first railroad was completed in Britain in 1830. The basis of our entire modern communication system was developed in the 19th century. And then modernisation spread across the world through industrialisation and colonisation. War technologies developed. The Industrial Revolution played a crucial role in shaping what we call the modern world.

## *The Age of Exploration*

The modern world started with the discoveries of new lands in America as well as new sea routes to countries like India. It started in Europe. Why did Europe have to do this, and how did it know that there was a world beyond, that there was something like Asia? How did it know about a country like India? The Muslims played an intermediary role in Europe knowing about the wider world. For example, the numeric system developed in India came to be known as Arabic numbers in Europe. The Europeans learnt them through the Arabs. The Europeans got to know about their past and heritage – science, philosophy, technology, and political systems – through the works preserved by the Muslims. These works had been translated from Greek and Latin to Arabic and Persian and later to Italian and other European languages. The Europeans took immense interest in them, which led to many creative changes called Renaissance.

The Europeans started exploring the world. They also wanted to find new sea routes to Asian and African countries because they were facing some problems with the existing land trade routes. In 1453, Constantinople, the capital of the Byzantine Empire, fell into the hands of the Ottomans, who were Muslims and who started creating problems for the Europeans. The Europeans wanted to avoid travelling through Turkey. So they wanted to find a new direct sea route to the East. By that time, navigational technologies also improved. The European explorations were led by the Portuguese and the Spanish. Then came the Dutch, the English and others.

Christopher Columbus thought of getting to India by heading westwards in the Atlantic Ocean but discovered America instead. The man who a few years later made it to India through a sea route was Vasco da Gama. He sailed around the tip of Africa and reached India in 1498. By 1510, the Portuguese were in Goa and established trade.

## *The Scientific Revolution*

The Scientific Revolution had two aspects, one aspect was purely related to science and the other was about the implications of this kind of thinking and reasoning for society as a whole and our understanding of the world.

The revolution began with Copernicus (1473–1543), a Polish astronomer. He established the heliocentric model, which said that the earth and other planets revolved around the sun. Following the Bible, people of that time believed that the earth was at the centre of the universe, which was called the geocentric model. Copernicus published his Revolution of Heavenly Bodies in the year of his death. He knew that Earth revolved around the sun years before, but he didn't want to get into any conflict with the Church. He published it only when he was approaching death. The heliocentric model was such a radical idea that even reformists like Luther and Calvin ridiculed it.

Copernicus's discovery had implications beyond science. It also meant that the Bible could be wrong and the Church could be wrong – they were not infallible anymore. They could be proven wrong through reasoning and questioning. This controverting of religion was one of the landmark developments in the history of modernisation.

Next came Kepler (1571–1630), a German astronomer, who formulated the three laws of celestial mechanics, called Kepler's laws, reinforcing the heliocentric model. Then came Galileo Galilei (1564–1642), an Italian astronomer, who became the first person to look at heavenly bodies with the aid of a telescope. These direct observations further helped in overthrowing Aristotle's geocentric system as endorsed by the Bible. However, the Church forced Galileo to confess that he was wrong. Then came Isaac Newton (1642–1727), whose work Principia Mathematica (1687) laid out the laws of motion and the law of gravity, establishing the new field of physics. Many developments took place in other fields of science as well, in chemistry, biology and so on.

## The Age of Enlightenment

The Scientific Revolution gave rise to rational thinking in many areas of life and society, which brought about what is called the Age of Enlightenment. There took place some major political revolutions at this time, during the 17th and 18th centuries. Many great thinkers and philosophers inspired the ethos of this age. French philosophers Voltaire and Rousseau inspired the French Revolution. Earlier, Thomas Hobbes and John Locke contributed to the English Revolution. The American thinkers Thomas Jefferson and Benjamin Franklin were an integral part of the American Revolution. Then there were many other prominent philosophers such as Hume and Kant and thinkers in various fields such as Adam Smith in economics.

The Industrial Revolution was an outcome of the Age of Enlightenment. The Industrial Revolution was also about new ways of thinking and reasoning, which involved designing new machines and experimenting with new political and economic ideas. These political revolutions as well as the Industrial revolution come under the Age of Enlightenment.

## Why in England first?

Why did the Industrial Revolution take place in England first? Such a revolution called for advancement in agricultural practices as a prerequisite. Agricultural productivity had to go up, only then fewer people would be tied to agriculture and the remaining people would be free to be occupied in other activities. New colonies gave opportunities for new crops to England. With new crops, hybrid seeds and fertilisers, agricultural productivity went up. There was three times more grain during the decade of the 1830s in England than in the whole previous century there. The population of England quadrupled between 1750 and 1850, as there was more food now and improvements in sanitation and vaccination.

There was growing international trade, there was paper money, and there was also the stock market. There was growing managerial expertise. Trade and merchant classes played an essential role in these developments. England's colonies were spread across the world. It had adequate capital for investment. The Bank of England existed since 1603. The economic philosophy in England at that time was that of non-interference of government in business. There were lower tariffs in England, to facilitate imports. Government funds were allotted to lay roads and build canals for ease of transport.

The stock market or non-interference in business, or government funds for transport –are all related to politics. Because of the Glorious Revolution, the political power shifted to the parliament from the monarchy. The parliament consisted of landlords and businessmen, who were able to formulate policies that were favourable to business and economic growth in England. Thus democracy created the right milieu for the Industrial Revolution and England became the leading force in industrialisation, while France and other countries burdened with monarchies lagged. The Industrial Revolution was fueled by steam power, and there was a popular saying at that time that "Steam is an Englishman."

Further, England had many rivers connected by canals, which made internal transport very convenient. The steamship was first made in 1816. Thus a favourable political system, the degree of importance given to the business class, the right economic ideology, having several colonies, availability of raw materials within the British territory itself, chiefly coal and iron, and the canals – all these factors made the Industrial Revolution possible in England before it could happen in other countries.

Also, Britain maintained its industrial techniques as state secrets. The knowledge of machine design and technology spread to Western Europe and the US from Britain only after about 1820. This way Britain could retain a monopoly over many things for about 70 years.

## *On democracy*

Democracy became possible only because of the Industrial Revolution. Industrialisation empowered people in many ways. Before the Industrial Revolution, people were confined to their communities and were tied to their families. The Industrial Revolution brought about factories and cities. It brought masses of people together. It gave rise to different classes of people and there was considerable mobility across these classes. The workers could come together, organise themselves and raise issues with the management. The power started shifting from non-working or idle classes to the working classes.

People started making demands for their rights. The adult franchise or the right to vote became important. Women did not have the right to vote for many decades, but later they could get it. There was a great deal of migration from rural areas to urban areas. In many urban areas and around factories in towns the living conditions were poor. There weren't any welfare measures at that time. There was poor sanitation. These things started to change gradually. The city life itself was a source of freedom. There were new professions, better incomes and people could live with dignity.

All these developments made the common people and workers demand rights. The traditional, conservative, hierarchical system with little opportunity for people to improve their lives was all shattered. These changes at the societal level created the right conditions for democracy.

## *Second Industrial Revolution*

The Industrial Revolution continued, but from the mid-nineteenth century onwards it was called the Second Industrial Revolution. It was of greater scale and scope and also had some different characteristics. The Industrial Revolution began with harnessing steam power, but during the Second Industrial Revolution, petroleum and electricity were the dominant sources of energy. This second revolution began in the 1850s and lasted till around 1920.

In the 1870s, German, American, English, and French inventors developed generators and transformers. Electric railways came by the 1890s. The internal combustion engine run on petroleum was invented in 1876. Automobiles came in the 1880s. Such inventions led to the formation of many new companies. The structure of these companies too changed. The ownership and management of these companies were separated, which enabled the rise of larger companies. Earlier, between 1760 and 1860, the private partnership was the standard form of a company, the ownership was limited to a few people. But from the 1860s, there were more and more joint stock companies where common people could own the stock of a company.

During the Second Industrial Revolution, the leadership role in industrialisation shifted from Britain to the US. America led the capitalist world, and with growing levels of industrialisation and modernisation, the lives of workers too kept improving. By 1914, there were better conditions for workers in most countries as compared to some decades earlier.

By the last quarter of the 19$^{th}$ century, all the males in most European countries got the right to vote. Illiterate and ignorant people too had equal right to vote as educated and socially aware people. The role of political campaigning increased and political parties became important.

## *Early socialists*

The Industrial Revolution at first gave rise to what was an early form of capitalism. Responding to it, some thinkers came up with ideas which would be called socialist. These were the people who called for more equality among people, better distribution of resources, and better working conditions for workers.

Marx and Engels called these early socialists such as Saint Simon and Robert Owen utopian socialists. These early socialists said that the situation was bad and had to be improved, a point on which Marx and Engels would agree. These early socialists felt all the people would come together in improving the society, including people from the upper classes, but Marx and Engels thought this was not possible.

Marx and Engels thought that there is a class conflict. According to them, the people from the working classes will get poorer and more miserable and so one day they will revolt against the capitalists. Marx and Engels called their version of socialism scientific socialism because they thought their views were based on a scientific analysis of history.

Engels in his book Socialism: Utopian and Scientific (1892) summarised his and Marx's position on utopian socialists: "The undeveloped state of the class struggle, as well as their own surroundings, causes socialists of this kind to consider themselves far superior to all class antagonisms. They want to improve the condition of every member of society, even that of the most favoured. Hence, they habitually appeal to society at large, without distinction of class; nay, by preference, to the ruling class. For how can people, when once they understand their system, fail to see it in the best possible plan of the best possible state of society? Hence, they reject all political, and especially all revolutionary, action; they wish to attain their ends by peaceful means, and endeavour, by small experiments, necessarily doomed to failure, and by the force of example, to pave the way for the new social gospel."

## *Saint-Simon*

One of the early socialists was Saint-Simon (1760–1825). Saint-Simon influenced many other socialists and thinkers, including Proudhon, Mill, Marx, Engels, and Veblen. He was imprisoned during the French Revolution for some time!

Saint-Simon

Saint-Simon argued that there are two classes, the industrial class and the idling class. In the context of the French Revolution, the nobility and the clergy in the French society constituted the idling classes, while all others, people who had to work for a living, came under the industrial classes. The industrial classes did not mean only manual labourers. The capitalists who worked came under the industrial class, and scientists came under the industrial class, as did managers. Saint-Simon proposed that the government should promote industrial classes and reduce idleness in society.

Saint-Simon called for hierarchical, merit-based organisation, which meant bureaucracy. He said that the working of a society should be based on a scientific understanding of man and society. "The astronomers only accepted those facts which were verified by observation; they chose the system which linked them best, and since that time, they have never led science astray."

Influenced by Adam Smith, he advocated less interference from the government in the economy. He wanted to adopt a scientific approach to promote the welfare of workers.

Saint-Simon believed that the system should work for the less privileged. He wrote in his book The New Christianity, "The whole of society ought to strive towards the amelioration of the moral and physical existence of the poorest class; society ought to organize itself in the way best adapted for attaining this end." Socialism to Saint-Simon was not about owning the means of production, nor was it about the class conflict, but was about designing the social system in such a way that the poorest are taken care of, and this had to be done scientifically or rationally.

## *Robert Owen*

Robert Owen (1771–1858) became wealthy through a textile mill at New Lanark, Scotland. He was very progressive. He offered much better working conditions and yet made this mill a very profitable business for him. He supported child labour legislation and free schools. He said, "The character is formed for and not by the individual" – which meant a person's character is a result of circumstances and as such education is very important. At that time, there were no schools and education and most children from the working classes were made to work for many hours. In Owen's company, however, the children of the workers were being educated. In 1817, Owen coined the slogan: "Eight hours' labour, eight hours recreation, eight hours' rest."

Robert Owen

At one time, 7-year olds would work for 12 to 13 hours a day. The Factory Acts of 1819 and 1833 limited the employment of children. But it was still legal for a 9-year-old to work for 8 hours per day.

Robert Owen had bigger ideas too, which made him get closer to the core ideals of socialism. He felt that society should be organised in the form of communes. This is his idea about how communes should be built: About 1200 people would settle on 1000 to 1500 acres, they would have a common kitchen, the parents are to raise their children only up to age 3 and after that, they are to have only occasional access to their children. Owen envisaged the entire society as consisting of such communes, with no private property. Even the upbringing and socialisation of children is also not a family business. He said of these communes: "Unions of them federatively united shall be formed in a circle of tens, hundreds and thousands." These communes will be interconnected based on common interests.

This was a radical idea, and Owen tried to implement a commune in the US. In 1824, he moved to the US and got a chance to address the US Congress in 1825, outlining his ideas on socialism. Robert Owen then set up a socialistic community in New Harmony, Indiana. He attracted over a thousand people. The commune lasted for 2 years and was dissolved in 1827.

It was a failed experiment, and Owen returned to London in 1828. Why did it fail? Because many kinds of people came there – scientists, educationists, workers and so on – but all were given the same privileges and facilities. Some people worked and many didn't work, there was no incentive system, and some felt that others were simply lazy. After Owen, there were some more communal experiments based on his ideas. However, till now no such experiment turned out to be a successful one.

Are Marx and Engels justified in calling Robert Owen a utopian socialist while calling themselves scientific socialists? Owen experimented with socialism and through such experimentation proved that it was not feasible. Owen's community experiment should have shown everyone, including Marx and Engels, that there were inherent problems with socialism and communism.

## *Think on it*

1. When did the Industrial Revolution take place?
2. How did the Industrial Revolution contribute to the modernisation of the world?
3. What is the Renaissance? What is its significance?
4. Why did the Europeans start exploring new sea routes?
5. How was the geocentric view of the universe challenged?
6. When did the Scientific Revolution begin?
7. What is meant by the Age of Enlightenment?
8. Why did the Industrial Revolution start in England?
9. How did the Industrial Revolution contribute to democracy?
10. What were some features of the Second Industrial Revolution?
11. Who were the early socialists? Why were they called utopian socialists?

12. What are the salient ideas of Saint-Simon?
13. What does the failure of communal living in the experiments of Robert Owen show?

# 20th Century

CHAPTER SIX

# World War I

World War I was most devastating, no country could have foreseen the nature and scale of this war. Many soldiers went to the war with great zeal. But the brutality of the war that they faced was shocking. By the end of it, over ten million soldiers died and twenty million were crippled or seriously injured. A huge part of the world was involved to some extent or other in this war. The scale, the level of mobilisation, and the ruthlessness with which people fought were all unprecedented. In the end, the people who started the war lost the war and lost a great deal with it, and the countries which won the war too didn't gain anything much.

The countries involved in the war did not expect what was to come. They were still thinking in terms of traditional wars with much fewer casualties. Why did this war cause so much destruction? Because the world changed in many important ways by the early twentieth century. The first thing that enlarged the scale of the war was colonialism. The colonies were dragged into the war. Then there was the factor of nationalism. Before nationalism emerged in the century or so preceding the First World War, in Europe and elsewhere, people lived in kingdoms or states. In a state, the people did not have a sense of identity or oneness with it. But the sense of oneness that a nation engendered meant easier mobilisation of people on a larger scale to fight the enemy. The next factor was the level of technology. There was new war machinery that could cause enormous destruction.

The victors held Germany solely responsible for starting the war. Historians agree that Germany played a very significant role in starting the war, under the leadership of Kaiser Wilhelm II. But if Kaiser's Germany hadn't started the war in 1914, could somebody else have started the war sometime later? Was war inevitable? Some historians believe that there were certain structural reasons why World War I took place, and so the war would have happened even if Germany hadn't become aggressive.

## *Thucydides' trap*

There is an important concept in political science that could explain the origins of World War I, called Thucydides' trap it was propounded by Graham Allison. It states that when there are two powers, with one of them being the ruling power and the other being an emerging power, there is always a possibility of conflict between these two. The ruling power wants to maintain the status quo, whereas the challenger wants to undermine it. By the early twentieth century, Britain was the greatest power on the earth and Germany was the challenger. Britain had the world under its control, and Germany had been emerging as a nation and it wanted to undermine the existing order.

Thucydides was a Greek thinker who said while explaining the Peloponnesian War that it was the rise of Athens and the fear it generated in Sparta that made the war inevitable. The established power may want to crush a rising power or the rising power may seek to be at the top. If Thucydides' trap is a valid assumption, then Germany was bound to challenge Britain at some point or other even if it didn't do it first, Britain was bound to attempt to crush it. So even if the war hadn't been started by Germany, Britain itself could have started it.

## *Unification of the Germans*

How did Britain come to be the foremost power in the world? The Glorious Revolution first changed Britain's polity, and then the Industrial Revolution happened first in Britain, taking a long time to spread to other nations. Britain also acquired many colonies. It became more powerful than France. For example, when Britain was trying to make India a colony, it was competing with the French, and Germany was nowhere around.

Britain and France were the major powers in Europe in the mid-nineteenth century. Britain had an advanced navy. But Germany was not even a nation yet. The Germans were spread across 16 kingdoms and city-states. There was a sectarian conflict between Catholics on the southern side and Protestants on the northern side. And there was opposition from the Austrian empire to the German unification. The Austrian opposition and the sectarian conflict prevented Germany from becoming one nation.

The man responsible for German unification was Otto von Bismarck, who was the chancellor of Wilhelm I, the Prussian king from 1861. The king and the chancellor, through a series of political moves, created a unified Germany with Berlin as its capital. They went to war with Austria in 1866 and won the war but instead of taking some territories from Austria, they wanted Austria not to interfere in the creation of a unified Germany. A confederation of northern German states was then created.

In 1871, there was a war between Germany and France. Bismarck made sure that it was France that invaded Germany, and earlier too he made sure that it was Austria that invaded Prussia. Bismarck felt that the Germans should feel that they were being threatened. France lost the war. Germany took Alsace and Lorraine, which were the sources of iron and coal to France. During the war with France, southern German states joined the northern German confederation. The new unified Germany came into being with 70 million inhabitants.

Germany became a nation, but Bismarck knew France was too powerful, so two resource-rich areas were taken away from France. Then he allied with the Austrian empire. He was on good terms with Russia. He also convinced Italy, which also became a nation recently, to be on Germany's side. Bismarck could thus balance Germany's power with that of France.

## *Alliances*

Kaiser Wilhelm II came to occupy the throne in 1888 and he was a very reckless person. He believed in militarism. He didn't like Bismarck's power. He wanted to decide things. In 1890, he dismissed Bismarck.

Kaiser Wilhelm II did not understand how the balance of power was maintained under Bismarck's tenure. He antagonised Russia. He started developing a navy to challenge Britain. Britain knew that Wilhelm II's Germany would challenge its power. Now Britain considered Germany to be its chief enemy rather than France. It entered into alliances with France and Russia, though both these countries had been its traditional enemies.

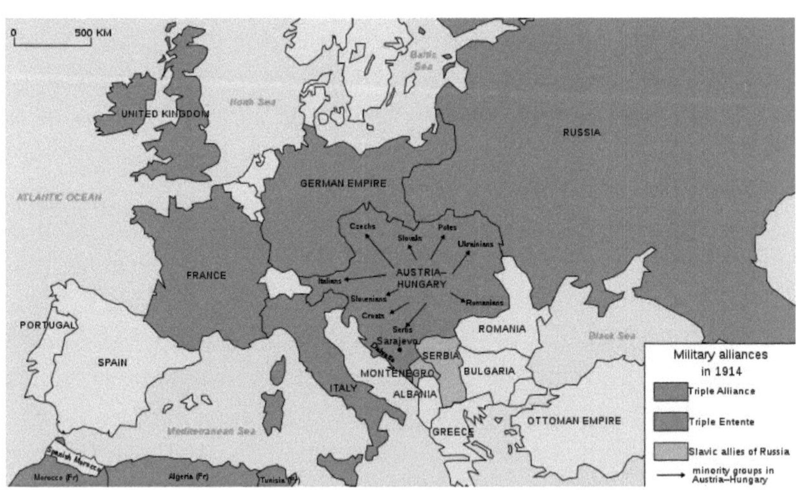


Alliances

Earlier, the triple alliance of Germany, Austria and Italy was formed during Bismarck's time in 1882. In 1893-94, the alliance of Russia and France was formed. In 1904, there was an Anglo-French entente. In 1907, there was an Anglo-Russian agreement. By 1907, Germany, Austria and Italy were pitted against Britain, France and Russia.

## *The events*

World War I was triggered by a small event, but it is in no way considered a cause. The heir to the Austrian throne, Archduke Franz Ferdinand, was assassinated in Sarajevo by a Serbian nationalist on June 28, 1914. Austria-Hungary was an empire consisting of Germans, Hungarians, Czechs, Slovaks, Poles, Ukrainians and Italians.

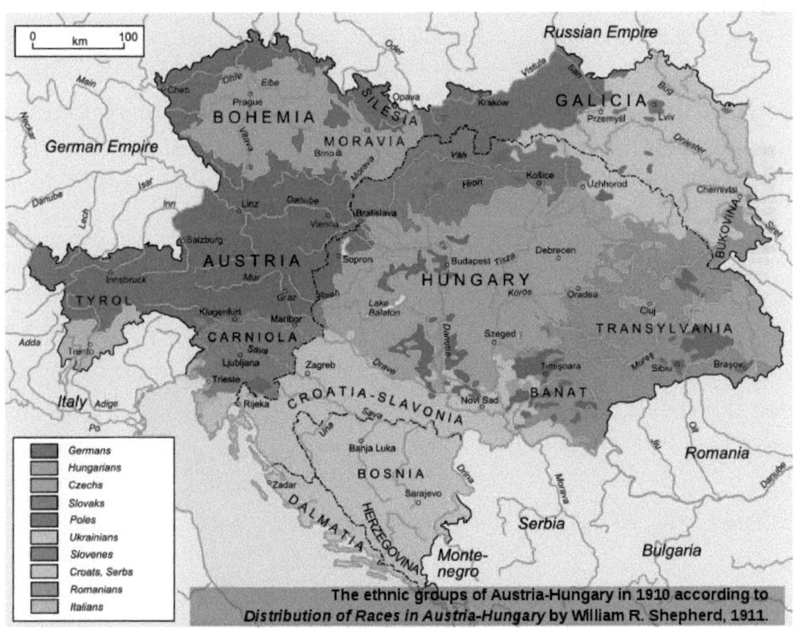

The ethnic groups of Austria-Hungary in 1910 according to *Distribution of Races in Austria-Hungary* by William R. Shepherd, 1911.

Austrian Empire

This assassination took place in Sarajevo, perpetrated by a Serbian nationalist who wanted this region to be a part of Serbia. This action was supported by Serbia. Austria thought of teaching a lesson to Serbia, and it was supported by Germany. If there was a war between Austria and Serbia, Russia might come to Serbia's defence.

Germany wanted to use this occasion to its advantage. It wanted Austria to go to war and wanted it to do so immediately so that Russia would not have enough time. Germany then wanted to invade France, through Belgium, but Belgium was a neutral country supported by Britain. Germany asked Belgium to permit troop movements, Belgium refused, but the Germans went through Belgium committing many atrocities on the way. Britain entered the war in defence of Belgium.

Germany, Austria and Italy were called the Central Powers, while Britain, France and Russia were called the Allies or Entente. During the war, Italy left the side of Germany and joined the Allied Powers. In 1917, Russia got out of the war due to the revolution there. The same year the US entered the war in support of the Allies. Germany had been sinking some American submarines which provoked the US.

Battles took place on the western front and the eastern front, which indicated the sides of France and Russia. There were also battles going on in Italy and Africa. By the end of the war, the Austria-Hungary empire disintegrated. The Ottoman Empire which had flourished for centuries, with Turkey as its centre, too came to an end.

## *Woodrow Wilson's 14 points*

After the US entered the war, it was an unequal fight between the Allies and the Central Powers. Germany lost. Many wanted to punish Germany. But Woodrow Wilson, the American president, who was once a political science professor, made some proposals to create a war-free world. He said there should be peace but without any victors. All the defeated countries, including Germany, would be treated fairly.

Woodrow Wilson

On January 8, 1918, Woodrow Wilson advanced fourteen points as a way forward in the post-war world. These points were the result of research done by 150 academics and had an idealistic tinge.

The first four points are:

1. No secret treaties.
2. Freedom of navigation on the seas

(3) Removal of economic barriers

(4) Reduction of armaments

The 5th point is that colonial disputes are to be settled by taking the people into account. This meant that the people who were under colonial powers had to be given importance. Wilson however didn't say that there should be decolonisation.

Points 6, 7, 8, and 11 deal with the restoration of invaded territories and compensation for damage. This was not only about Germany giving compensation to the countries it invaded but applied to any invading country.

Points 9, 10 and 12 are about Italy, Austria-Hungary, and the Ottoman Empire respectively, giving more importance to individual nationalities.

Point 13 deals with Poland, areas with Polish populations are to be given back to Poland.

The 14th point deals with the creation of the League of Nations.

Woodrow Wilson tried to give power and independence to the various nationalities in Europe, though he ignored the nations in Asia and Africa and their right to self-rule. He believed that a just world is a solution to the problem of war. Coming from an American president, this was a very rare thing. He could take that position because he was an idealist by nature and also because America was not particularly involved in European disputes. He came closer to being Plato's ideal of philosopher-king than any other ruler of that time. The other leaders wanted revenge, they wanted to punish Germany as much as possible. During the wartime, the leaders promised many things to their people about crushing Germany, and in the end if you let Germany go unpunished, what would they tell their people?

## *Treaty of Versailles*

The Treaty of Versailles signed in 1919 was so different from Woodrow Wilson's idealism. As per this treaty:

– Germany should accept full responsibility for starting the war. It should pay $33 billion to the victors (12 times higher in 2012, when adjusted for inflation).

– Alsace and Lorraine, which Germany took away in 1871, would be given back to France. Germany lost 10% of its land and population to Poland and Czechoslovakia. It lost all its overseas possessions.

– Size of the German army was not to cross 100,000. It can have no submarines and no air force. Rhineland, which bordered France, is not to be militarised.

– Austria is forbidden to join Germany. After the collapse of the Austrian empire, its populations were allotted to different nations. But Germans in Austria could not become part of Germany. Millions of Germans came under Czech rule. Polish borders were redrawn and comprised areas with German populations.

Most historians think that the Treaty of Versailles was the reason for World War II. They say it was unfair. It ended up antagonising Germany, provoking more nationalism there and was finally responsible for the rise of Hitler. Woodrow Wilson could foresee this and said after the treaty was signed that there would be another world war within a generation.

After the treaty, the economist J.M. Keynes said, “Next war would come in 20 years.” World War II started exactly in 1939. Keynes attended the Versailles Conference as a delegate of the British treasury. He was not a famous economist at that time. He became famous during the inter-war period. Keynes looked at the world from an economic point of view, he thought of an interdependent and integrated Europe as a solution to the war. He did not want Germany to be punished and pay huge war reparations. If other countries of Europe had to grow, Germany also had to prosper.

Keynes calculated that the amount of compensation Germans had to pay would make them suffer a lot. He said that if a man suffers beyond a point, “he listens to whatever instruction of hope, illusion, or revenge is carried to them in the air.” Indeed Hitler would come carrying revenge in the air. Keynes said these things in the book he wrote in 1919, The Economic Consequences of Peace. He was critical of everybody, including Woodrow Wilson. On Wilson, he said, "The collapse of the president has been one of the decisive moral events of the history." Keynes thought the treaty was unfair, immoral and foolish.

Was Keynes right in his calculations about the coming of WW II? Not entirely, World War II took place not simply due to the treaty but also due to Great Depression, which no one, including Keynes, predicted. But others thought that if you wanted to crush Germany, the treaty did not do a good enough job of it. Germany should have been divided, they said. Perhaps that would have prevented WW II.

After World War II, the reconstruction of Europe started under the Marshall Plan. Also, the United Nations was created, and it was stronger than the League of Nations. Some institutions such as the IMF and the World Bank were developed to facilitate world cooperation. Germany was also divided.

One way to think about the Treaty of Versailles is that it was unfair and so provoked Germany to rise again, another view is that the treaty was not harsh enough to crush Germany. After World War II, in a way, they implemented both the fair and harsh approaches and indeed World War III did not happen. Germany was helped to rebuild itself, but it was also divided.

After the First World War, the Austria-Hungary empire became Austria, Hungary, Czechoslovakia, Poland, and Yugoslavia. And also Europe's outlying Turkish empire dissolved, with the core area coming under Mustafa Kemal's military dictatorship. Thereafter Jordan, Palestine, Iraq, Syria, Arabia and Lebanon became French or British protectorates, which more or less meant colonies.

## *Think on it*

1. What is Thucydides' trap?
2. What was the position of the Germans before their unification under Bismarck?
3. How did Bismarck bring about the unification of the Germans?
4. Mention the European alliances formed before World War I.
5. Explain how one relatively small event brought about the involvement of many nations at the outset of WW I.

6. What are Woodrow Wilson's 14 points for the post-war world?
7. Why were Woodrow Wilson's points rejected by the other world leaders?
8. What are the salient aspects of the Treaty of Versailles?
9. What are the arguments of Keynes against the Treaty of Versailles?
10. What happened to Austria-Hungary and Ottoman empires at the end of World War I?

CHAPTER SEVEN

# Russian Revolution

A revolution is a sweeping and sudden social change, it need not be a positive change always, it can also be negative. Russian Revolution was an important development not just for Russia but also for the whole world. It inspired the world, and it gave the impression to the world this is how Marxism is to be implemented. It provided a template for any country seeking to bring about communism and Marxism. The person who gave this template was Lenin. But there was something fundamentally wrong about it.

There is absolutely no doubt now in the minds of historians that the experiment that took place in the USSR was a major disaster. We need to know how it turned out to be so. Marx predicted that communism would become a reality in some advanced capitalist countries first, in countries such as Germany, France or England, but he never foresaw that it could happen in a country like Russia. Russia was primarily agrarian and feudal. According to Marx, feudalism would die and give way to capitalism, and as that capitalism grows and reaches an advanced stage, it would pave way for communism.

At such an advanced capitalist stage, Marx thought, the society would be divided only into two classes, a few capitalists on one side and a large proletariat in a miserable condition on the other side. Proletariat means the industrial working class. This proletariat would rebel and establish communism, abolishing private property.

## *1905 revolution*

Czars were the autocratic rulers of Russia. In the Crimean War of 1853-56, Britain and France defeated Russia. Because of this humiliation, the Czar wanted to make Russia more progressive and powerful. Serfdom was abolished in 1861 to create more labour flexibility, and not for any humanitarian reasons. The land allotted to a freed serf was not enough for him to become a farmer. Still, it was a limited reform.

Russia went through a phase of massive industrialisation between 1900 to 1930. It was started during the time of Czar Nicholas II, who ruled between 1894 and 1917 and during whose regime both the 1905 revolution and the 1917 revolution took place. By 1905, there was great unrest all around Russia. The peasants were suffering. The industrial workers were suffering. And then there had been a war with Japan in 1904 in which Russia was defeated. This was the first time a European country got defeated by an Asian or non-Western country.

The war with Japan triggered the 1905 revolution. The war with Germany, during the First World War, triggered the 1917 revolution. Both these wars shattered the myth of the power of the government. They brought great suffering to the people. The discontented people became more assertive. On January 22, 1905, when a large group of people gathered only to petition the Czar, they were fired upon, and hundreds were killed. This came to be called Bloody Sunday. It started a wave of unrest across the country. The Czar then introduced certain reforms. They included a parliamentary government based on a constitution. This parliament with democratically elected members was called Duma. But over the years, this government became too weak, the Czar came to be powerful. People thought of democracy as the only alternative to autocracy and at that time they didn't think of communism, though a few were working on it.

## *1917 revolution before Lenin*

Russia got involved in World War I, though it was completely unprepared for it. It could have chosen not to join the war, but the Czar was not prudent enough to take that option. Its performance in the war was disastrous. A large number of Russian soldiers died. And the condition within the country went on to deteriorate. There was a shortage of food which caused bread riots. The troops refused to fire on the rioting people this time. In 1905, the troops were loyal to the Czar, but in 1917 they were not. There were agitations all over the country, and the Czar abdicated the throne.

A committee of the Duma created a provisional government which was led by Alexander Kerensky. This government could not decide to exit the war. It had a plan to draft a constitution by an elected constituent assembly.

There was another important development at this time. Workers and soldiers were creating what were called Soviets. They were hierarchically arranged councils which facilitated local self-government. Also, around this time, peasants at some places started seizing farms from their owners.

## *Lenin enters*

Vladimir Lenin (1870–1924) had his own ideas about communism. To both Marx and Lenin, communism meant a society where there is no private property, but Marx thought it would come about naturally through an evolutionary process while Lenin believed in the creation of a communist society through a revolution.

How did Lenin become a revolutionary? His brother was executed for his role in a plot to kill the Czar. We would have called him a terrorist. This kind of terrorist might think some major change would come if the ruler is eliminated. His brother could have asked for pardon and become free but he did not do so. Lenin was inspired by his brother, he studied Marxism and looked at the Russian situation from a Marxist point of view. He wanted to apply

Marxism to the Russian situation and change the society, rather than simply try to eliminate a ruler.

Vladimir Lenin

Lenin then got involved in certain anti-state activities because of which he was exiled. By 1917, he had been in exile for almost twenty years. He was in Switzerland when changes started happening in Russia. Lenin hoped Russia would be defeated in the war so that the revolution could happen more quickly. In April 1917, Germany helped Lenin move from Switzerland to Russia, secretly, as the Germans thought Lenin's presence in Russia would create trouble there.

## *October Revolution*

After Lenin came to Russia, he made some big promises to the people. His slogan was "Land, bread, peace." Also, "All power to the Soviets." He assured the people about the restoration of safety and security in the country. There would be food again. The soldiers and the workers felt they would get power through the Soviets. Lenin also promised land. The landless peasants would have thought that they would all get a piece of land.

Lenin belonged to the Social Democratic Party. It was split into two factions. Lenin's faction came to be called Bolsheviks and the other side was Mensheviks. The Mensheviks believed the situation was not right for the communist revolution because Russia was a primarily agrarian society, but Lenin wanted to make communism happen. Lenin wanted to seize power at any cost.

Marx himself said that the communist revolution did not have to mean only a proletarian revolution, there can be a bourgeois revolution first which could then facilitate the proletarian revolution. Lenin thought that there had been such an opportunity to create a revolution in Russia in 1905. It was not made use of. He was not expecting another opportunity in his lifetime, but when it came, he didn't want to miss it.

In 1917, Lenin was a leader for only about 100,000 people in a population of 160 million. The urban working class constituted 5% of the population while the peasantry made up 80% of it. Through his promises and rhetoric, Lenin got in tune with the mood of the masses. He staged a coup on the provisional government, in which a few hundred people died. It happened on October 26, 1917, according to the Russian calendar, which was the old calendar. It was called the October Revolution. The actual date of it was November 6. What happened on that day was a relatively small event compared to many things that would happen after it. St Petersburg was the capital of Russia at that time and not Moscow. Workers and soldiers in St. Petersburg seized the government headquarters and the provisional government was ousted.

Lenin signed the peace treaty of Brest-Litovsk, in March 1918. Russia had to give some of its industrial and fertile regions to

Germany. George Orwell once said, "The shortest way to end a war is to lose it," and Lenin did not mind losing the war, he just wanted to end it.

But there were also supporters of the war in Russia, who formed a group called Whites, and the Bolsheviks came to be called Reds. There was a civil war between them. As Lenin was pulling Russia out of war, the Allied Powers opposed Lenin. Lenin also cancelled foreign debt; the British and the French would lose heavily. The Allies sent 100,000 troops to Russia in support of the Whites. Trotsky led the Reds. He was the most important Bolshevik leader after Lenin. He was also regarded as an intellectual, he wrote books and was known outside Russia.

Lenin abolished the constituent assembly. The Bolsheviks were not popular in the constituent assembly. Moreover, Lenin did not want to give any role to the constituent assembly. Large industrial houses were taken over by the new government and banks were nationalised. The peasants initially got lands, but later Lenin introduced collectivisation. He wanted all the agricultural land to be managed by the party through collective farms. Now he was not giving land, he was taking it away from all the peasants. The communist revolution was at first presented as poor peasants revolting against the rich landlords, but later it became a war against the poor also.

During the civil war, the Red Army was forcibly taking grain from the peasants. Lenin said whoever could give should give, a family could keep just enough grain for its use and not more. Anybody who was hoarding was declared an enemy. These were all unpopular measures, which created discontent in the populace. Lenin had to maintain strong secret police, Cheka, to deal with any kind of opposition or resistance. The Army first got divided into Reds and Whites and then all of it became the Red Army. All the powers of the government were taken over by the party. The Bolsheviks became the Communist Party in 1918, and all other parties were banned by 1922.

Lenin and a very few people under him were doing all this. Land was promised to the peasants but subsequently all land was taken away from them. Power was promised to the Soviets, but they did not get any power. In March 1921, the sailors at Kronstadt naval base rebelled against the government, and these were the people who had supported Lenin at the time of the revolution. The Red Army suppressed this rebellion. All the power in the country was held by the party, and the party was led by one man, Lenin. The police and the army were under Lenin and whoever opposed him got eliminated.

## *New Economic Policy*

By 1921, four years into the revolution, Lenin understood that many things were going wrong. He wanted to take one step back. The chaos he created was proving disastrous for the economy. He then introduced what is called the New Economic Policy (NEP).

In 1921, the Russian GDP was 20% of what it was in 1913. It was a huge fall because the incentive systems were disrupted. Under the NEP, Lenin allowed small-scale businesses to be in private hands. Earlier he had nationalised everything. Now, he said only the "commanding heights" would be with the state.

Lenin died in 1924. By 1928, the agrarian and industrial sectors made a stunning recovery. The degree of liberalisation was so much that some thought Bolshevism's bark was much worse than its bite. Some people thought that Lenin understood his mistake and tried to set things straight again. Deng, the future president of China, was on a visit to Russia at this time and he saw how capitalism could cause economic growth.

Lenin changed the economy when it was leading to disastrous results. But even then he did not change the political structure. Lenin died abruptly, in his early 50s. Had he lived longer, communism would have taken a different path.

## *Stalin*

The general secretary of the Communist Party at the time of Lenin's death was Stalin. Joseph Stalin (1878–1953) was far more ruthless than Lenin. He was very close to Lenin. Lenin used to give all kinds of dirty work to Stalin, like even bank robberies. The revolutionaries were getting money that way. Other jobs included snatching grains away from the farmers and settling the unrest of the people by killing some of them.

Joseph Stalin

Stalin was not seen as an intellectual, but as a solid worker, a strategist and a planner, in contrast to his top rival in the party, Trotsky. Stalin believed in Marxism as Lenin interpreted it. He thought he should implement what Lenin only tried to implement. Stalin moved forward where Lenin hesitated and dealt with things in a far more ruthless manner. Collectivisation was brutally forced on the peasants.

Workers would want communism but not farmers. Communism meant more power to the workers who did not have any share in the industry, but it was not so with the farmers. The farmers wanted land for themselves, not a share in land management. Collectivisation was very unpopular.

Stalin, like Lenin, believed in the power of rapid industrialisation for communism to succeed. He wanted to forcibly industrialise the country so that there would be a more industrial proletariat.

Stalin committed many atrocities in implementing his policies. The first kind of atrocity was simply to shoot and kill people. The next one was sending people to exile. People who went to exile might never return, mostly they would just die in the labour camps. Stalin systematically eliminated his opponents. He eliminated all his old comrades too. Even his family members were not spared, some of them committed suicide.

Stalin launched the Five Year Plans in 1928. Over 10 million people died during the collectivisation drive between 1929 and 1933. For comparison, ten million is the number of casualties in World War I. Most of them died due to famines. Famines were repeatedly happening because of the fall in agricultural production. And so many people were being sent to prison camps that around 10% of the 1930s GDP was produced by the prisoners.

Between 1936 and 1938, all of Lenin's associates were purged in a series of show trials where Stalin would make an accusation and they would have to confess in the hope that they may be given a life sentence rather than hanged or shot. They would confess but still, they would be killed. And millions of people were imprisoned. Between 1935 and 1953, the year of Stalin's death, around 10 million people were banished to prison camps. Most of them did not survive.

Stalin presided over a totalitarian regime, which combined personal dictatorship with adherence to an ideology. And it is more dangerous than personal dictatorship alone. If it was only a personal dictatorship, many people would try to rebel. An ideology on the other hand would enlist the cooperation of a great number of people because they would think that their leader is fighting for a higher cause. Stalin gave the impression that Russia was moving forward. Did it move forward? In a way, yes, the USSR became a major power in a short time, because of Stalin's efforts – but at what cost? Millions of people were dying, everybody lived in a constant nightmare, year after year, decade after decade.

From Marxism to Leninism, things took a huge turn in the direction of ruthlessness, and from Leninism to Stalinism, there was yet another turn in the same direction. Lenin might not have done many things Stalin did. Lenin sensed during his last days that Stalin could be far too vicious. He dictated a note alerting people about Stalin, but Stalin made that note disappear. Stalin projected himself as the obvious successor to Lenin. He glorified Lenin after his death and through that glorification fortified his own position.

Trotsky fled the country, but he was not spared. He was tracked and killed in Mexico by Stalin's men. Marx's vision of communism where everyone is expected to contribute as per one's capacity and take only as per one's need voluntarily as in a family when realised by Lenin and Stalin created one of the evilest and most ruthless states in the history of the world.

## *Think on it*

1. Why would an advanced capitalist state lead to communism, according to Marx?
2. When did the Crimean War take place? What is its outcome?
3. What events triggered the 1905 revolution?
4. How did the war with Japan contribute to the 1905 revolution?
5. What was the outcome of the 1905 revolution?
6. What events triggered the 1917 revolution?
7. What was the political situation of Russia in 1917 before Lenin entered the scene?
8. What promises did Lenin make to the people in 1917?
9. How did Lenin overthrow the provisional government?

10. What are the consequences of Russia withdrawing from World War I?
11. Why was there a civil war in Russia, after the 1917 revolution?
12. Why did Lenin introduce the collectivisation of agriculture?
13. What do you know about the rebellion at Kronstadt naval base?
14. Explain how Lenin concentrated all power in himself.
15. What is the role of the Communist Party in the former USSR?
16. How did Stalin come to power?
17. What were the economic policies of Stalin?
18. How did Stalin maintain his grip over power?

CHAPTER EIGHT

# Mussolini and Hitler

The ideology of fascism played a particularly important role in World War II. The template for implementing fascism was first given by Mussolini, and it was followed by Hitler. Mussolini showed the direction, and Hitler perfected it. Hitler was far more successful in creating a fascist state. A fascist state is also called a totalitarian state. Totalitarianism refers to the government's control over all the aspects of society, including the private lives of the people.

Fascism or totalitarianism is built around a dictator, but it is more than just a dictatorship or autocracy. It is autocracy combined with a particular ideology. It happened for the first time in Italy, under Mussolini. Italy, like Germany, was a recently formed nation. Till the mid-nineteenth century, the Italians were spread over many kingdoms and city-states. Italy became a single nation in 1870.

Both Italy and Germany were new nations. The people were developing a new sense of unity. This is a prerequisite for fascism, this sense of 'we-ness', like 'We Italians'. There is more scope for fascism if the people have a sense of pride in their past. Italy's past was the Roman Empire, one of the greatest empires in history. The Italians were beginning to think: 'We can regain the glory if only we act united, as one, under one leader.'

The word 'fascism' comes from the Latin word, 'fasces' which in Ancient Rome denoted a bundle of rods with an axe head. It represented that man had executive authority. A bundle of rods is stronger than a single rod. Individual rods are joined together and become one, one can say it is a loss of individuality. All people become one with a purpose. The concept behind fascism symbolised a power which individuals do not have as individuals but which they have as a group.

## *Mussolini's rise to power*

Benito Mussolini (1883–1945), had been a socialist and an editor of a socialist magazine. Socialism opposes war. But Mussolini started campaigning for the participation of Italy in World War I and was removed from the socialist party. Then he joined the war, subsequently, he got wounded and came out in 1917.

Benito Mussolini

During World War I, Italy switched sides, moving to the winning side. After the war, the Italians were upset by the peace treaty. Italy felt that though it won it did not get what it wanted. For example, Italy expected territorial additions to its colonies of Somalia and

Libya from the British and the French, but it did not get any.

At that time, the upper classes in Italy were fearing Bolshevism that was surging in Russia. The lower classes were facing many problems like unemployment. In 1922, Mussolini used this discontent to create a radical organisation of youth called Black Shirts. He created a large band of loyalists for himself. They were soon found in every Italian town. They stood for the greater glory of Italy. They were attacking Mussolini's opponents. They were creating lawlessness. Mussolini wanted to seize power by force from a weak government. He was making many promises to all classes of people.

The king of Italy, Victor Emmanuel III, was very weak. When the prime minister resigned and there was no clear alternative, the king decided to make Mussolini the premier. But Mussolini didn't want it to appear like a gift given by the king, so he organised his group of 30,000 Black Shirts to make what he called "March on Rome," as if they came to take over the power by force. Later Mussolini would claim 300,000 people took part in the march.

Mussolini ruled legally for two years. Then he rigged the 1924 elections, because of which the fascists got most votes in the parliament. His men started creating trouble for the opponents. Finally, those parties were forced to disband themselves. By 1926, Mussolini created a one-party state. He called himself 'II Duce', the leader. His following grew. His fans used slogans such as "Mussolini is always right," "Believe! Obey! Fight!" "Better to live one day as a lion than a hundred years like a sheep," "A minute on the battlefield is worth a lifetime of peace!" and "Nothing has ever been won in history without bloodshed."

Mussolini was mobilising the army and the people for war. While there had been unemployment previously, there was now more economic activity which created employment. There was new optimism, some of it genuine and some of it based on propaganda and suppression of opposition. This was the state that Mussolini created, which would become a template for Hitler.

## *Hitler's rise to power*

Adolf Hitler (1889–1945) was born in Austria. He took part in World War I as a soldier. In 1920, he took over a small political group called the National Socialist German Workers' Party (NSDAP), the members of which were called Nazis. In 1923, Hitler attempted a coup in Munich but failed. This was one year after Mussolini succeeded in coming to power in Italy. Hitler was arrested. He used his coup attempt to gain a name for himself. He spent only one year in jail, when he wrote his autobiographical work, Mein Kampf, meaning My Struggle. In 1924, the Nazi movement started gaining strength. But few took Hitler's ideas of the extermination of Jews seriously.

Adolf Hitler

Hitler stood for antisemitism, which means hatred of Jews, and for undoing the Versailles treaty. Many rich people in Germany supposedly made money during the First World War, some of them being Jews, and Hitler wanted to confiscate that money. Originally, he also had a socialist agenda, like protecting the middle classes from big business and also distributing land to the peasants.

Hitler's basic aim was to bring back the glory to the Germans and create a land of pure Aryans. There would be no Jews in this land of pure Aryans. Hitler held the German Jews to be responsible for Germany's debacle in World War I. He also said that the German leaders agreed to the Versailles treaty because of some conspiracy which involved Jews, though there was no evidence for any such thing.

Such talk of hatred tends to gain popularity during hard times. Hitler made little headway from 1925 to 1929 when the German economy was doing somewhat well. In 1928, the Nazis got only 2.6% of the vote and 12 seats in the Reichstag, the German parliament. But the collapse of the economy in 1930-31, due to the Great Depression, set the stage for the Nazi success. During that time, the American aid to Germany was cut off and Germany's international trade shrank. There was more than a 25% unemployment rate in Germany.

In 1930, the Nazis won 107 seats, which was the second largest. They moved from being nowhere to being the second largest party. In 1932 they became the single largest party, though they still lacked the majority. On Jan 30, 1933, President Paul von Hindenburg appointed Hitler as the chancellor.

Hitler applied the constitution's emergency provision citing an alleged communist plot to overthrow the new government. Using it, he crushed thousands of his opponents. Hitler called for another round of elections after he came to power, hoping to get a majority this time, but the Nazis again did not get it. Then Hitler arrested all communists and some others as traitors. He thus created a rump parliament and enacted the Enabling Act, giving the government the power to rule by decree during an emergency. All other parties were banned one by one. By mid-1933, the Nazis were the only legal political organisation in Germany. The party was now very large and growing, it had various subgroups, of women, youth, farmers, and so on.

Hitler also had to deal with his enemies in his own party. During his rise to power in the 20s, Hitler created two organisations modelled on Mussolini's Black Shirts, the paramilitary Storm Troops and his personal guard SS. Now he felt that some members of the Storm Troops were not loyal enough, so he simply wanted to eliminate them. They were asked to come to a particular venue on a particular day in June 1934, and they were all simply killed by the members of the SS. This was called the Night of the Long Knives.

Hitler got 400 to 1000 people of his own paramilitary force killed over 3 days. The Storm Troops had been posing a threat to the German army, Hitler got rid of his opponents in the Storm Troops with the assurance that the army would support him. Hitler then gained control over the army. The president died in 1934. Hitler became the only person at the head of everything in Germany.

Herman Goering was number 2 in the hierarchy of power. Heinrich Himmler was the head of the SS. Joseph Goebbels was the chief propagandist of the Nazi party. By the middle of the Second World War, about 1/5$^{th}$ of all adult Germans joined the Nazis, though some did so only under pressure.

## *Antisemitism*

Only Hitler had an anti-Jews attitude and not Mussolini. To Hitler, the German race had to be kept pure, it had to have more territory, and there had to be no presence of Jews in the new Germany.

The SS operated the concentration camps. The first one was set up in 1934, in Germany. Later there were others in the conquered territories. Hitler first got the Jews expelled from government jobs. The Nuremberg Laws of 1935 prohibited the Germans from having marriage or sex with the Jews. Hitler then forced the Jews to live in ghettos. The Nuremberg Laws, which were first passed in the context of the Jews, were later extended to gipsies, people of African descent, and even to those people who were mentally retarded or those with physical defects though they may be of Aryan stock. Hitler was interested in creating a pure as well as a strong German nation.

As Hitler was adding more and more territories to Germany, he had to deal with more Jews also. To him, it was 'the Jewish problem'. In 1942, he came up with what he called the final solution. The decision was to send the Jews from the ghettos to concentration camps in Poland. The idea was to gradually get rid of them, to gas them, to kill them.

By 1945, over 6 million Jews were killed. Only a few tens of thousands of the 2 million Jews in Germany in 1933 managed to survive. Germany got more than 4 million Jews from the conquered territories. In every territory Hitler occupied, the Jews were identified, separated and sent to the concentration camps.

Why did others allow this? Not many people knew what was going on. Also, the majority didn't care about the minority. Many Germans thought, 'we are not Jews. We are safe.'

## *World War II*

In 1933, the year Hitler came to power, Germany got out of the League of Nations. In 1935, Germany abrogated the Treaty of Versailles formally. Hitler started conscription for a larger army in violation of the treaty. Next, the air force was created.

In 1936, a small contingent of the German army was sent to Rhineland, which was supposed to be demilitarised. The German military generals were scared of what would happen if their soldiers were sent to Rhineland, they were afraid that France or Britain would attack them. But no such thing happened. This boosted the confidence of the Germans. It showed them that Hitler can take a chance and win. When people around him feared doing something, Hitler could dare to take the risk.

In 1938, Austria was annexed, and the Germans there welcomed Hitler. They wanted Austria to be a part of the emerging German power. The next move was a little riskier. There were some Germans living in Czechoslovakia, they were called Sudeten Germans. They were asked to agitate against the Czech government so that Hitler could say these Germans were being ill-treated and they should be a part of Germany. In September 1938, the British prime minister Chamberlain, the French leader Edouard Daladier, Mussolini and Hitler met in Munich. Hitler was allowed to take a part of Czechoslovakia into Germany. France could not help Czechoslovakia though it had a defence pact with it along with Poland and Romania.

Germany was ready to fight and the other countries were not. Britain and France were being lenient towards Hitler, this was called appeasement policy. Ironically, at this point, Stalin was willing to help France and Britain, he asked them not to yield to Hitler's demands. But they did not want to take Stalin's help. Just 6 months after taking a part of Czechoslovakia, Hitler moved to get the entire country.

In March 1939, Britain signed a pact with Poland guaranteeing British and French aid if Poland was attacked. On August 23, Hitler signed a nonaggression pact with Stalin. The agreement was if Stalin stayed neutral, he would get three Baltic states from Germany, as well as parts of Poland and Romania which once belonged to Russia. Some more areas would come under the Russian sphere of influence.

On Sept 1, 1939, Hitler launched what's called the German blitzkrieg – the lightning war – and invaded Poland. This attack was considered the beginning of the Second World War.

## *Think on it*

1. What is totalitarianism?
2. What is the origin of the word 'fascism'?
3. Why was Italy unhappy about the outcome of World War I?
4. Who were Black Shirts? What was their role in Mussolini's rise to power?
5. What was Mussolini's 'March on Rome'?
6. Who were the Nazis?

7. In what way did Hitler follow Mussolini?
8. What factors contributed to the rise of Hitler?
9. What were Storm Troops and SS?
10. What were Hitler's ideas about Jews?
11. What was Hitler's 'final solution ' to what he considered the Jewish problem?
12. How many Jews were killed by Hitler? How did he do it?
13. In what way did Hitler undermine the Treaty of Versailles?
14. What was meant by the appeasement policy of Britain and France before the Second World War?
15. What do you know about the Hitler-Stalin pact?
16. Trace the events that led to World War II.

CHAPTER NINE

# The Rise of Japan and World War II

The Second World War took place in European and Pacific theatres. In military parlance, a theatre is a region in which active military operations are carried out. Japan was the aggressor in the Pacific theatre and Germany in the European. Germany had an ally in Italy. Germany, Japan and Italy were called the Axis powers.

How did Japan come to this position where it could face the might of America in the Pacific? Japan developed very rapidly in just a few decades during the late nineteenth and early twentieth centuries and emerged as a powerful nation. Its path of progress was very unusual. Before Japan started becoming modern, it was a feudal society that used to be called the shogunate. The head of the shogunate was a shogun. And there was an emperor endowed with a semi-divine status.

The emperor held a high position but did not have many powers. The powers were exercised by the shogun. The country was divided into several domains, and each of them was ruled by a daimyo. In the last shogunate, there were around 200 domains.

There were professional warriors called samurai who worked for daimyo and shogun. The samurai constituted a caste, a samurai could not take up any other occupation. Then the Japanese society consisted of farmers, artisans and traders, the farmers occupying the highest position and the traders the lowest. Besides these three groups, some lower-class people were simply called commoners.

The samurai caste made up 7% of the population during the Tokugawa shogunate. Tokugawa Leyasu, who lived from 1542 to 1616, established the Tokugawa shogunate, which brought a new era of peace putting an end to a lot of fighting between various clans. His capital was Edo, which later became Tokyo, whereas the emperor ruled from Kyoto.

The Tokugawa shogunate, which lasted till the early 19th century, followed a policy of isolation which was called sakoku. Before this period of isolation, Japan had been open. In 1543, the Portuguese entered Japan, bringing Christianity with them. By 1600, around 300,000 Japanese became Christians. Under Tokugawa shogunate, however, those who were converted to Christianity were forced to convert back and the missionaries were sent away. Just some Dutch merchants were allowed to stay, and through these merchants, some people had access to science texts. During the Tokugawa shogunate, the importance of the samurai went down as there were not many wars. The traders became more important.

## *Meiji Revolution*

In the mid-nineteenth century, the Japanese realised that they would be colonised like many other countries in Asia unless something drastic was done. In 1853-54, Japan was forced to open up by US commodore Matthew Perry. This was a great humiliation for the Japanese. It was followed by unequal treaties with the US and other Western powers. The Western powers established ports against the will of the local people. The Americans had done the same thing in China before.

As the shogunate was too weak to stop foreign intervention, it was abolished and the Meiji ruled Japan between 1868 to 1912. Modernisation of the Japanese started during the Meiji rule, it was called the Meiji Revolution or the Meiji Restoration. Education was introduced, and there was mobility across the classes. The Japanese started building a navy, they wanted to be like a European power. Their development story started in 1870 and by 1904, in 35 years, they could attack Russia and win the war. It shocked the world. All these reforms were carried out by a group of leaders.

The daimyo domains were abolished in 1871. The samurai forces were disbanded, their privileges were taken away. Even their swords were taken away in 1876. The samurai were so proud of their swords. Several attempts by the samurai to rebel failed. The people were free to take up any occupation. The land was redistributed among the peasants. The land markets were developed, and the land could be mortgaged, sold and used as a proper investment. The peasants began to pay in cash to the government directly, earlier they were paying taxes in terms of services to the daimyo.

A new financial system of taxes, banks, and the currency was introduced. Transport, which included railways, was developed. Industrialisation took place. A new form of a company called Zaibatsu, which was a government-assisted large corporation, emerged.

By 1900, the government was providing 6 years of free education for most people. Hundreds of students were being sent abroad annually. Even before the Meiji Restoration, Japan's literacy rate was 40%, which was the highest in Asia.

A new constitution was framed in 1889. The right to vote was limited to 5% of men, to only those who had property or some high qualification. More power was given to the Meiji king. The Japanese constitution was based on the German constitution which was authored by Bismarck. The Japanese wanted to emulate Germany. The Shinto faith according to which the emperor was a semi-divine figure, a belief that was central to the Japanese culture, was not changed.

There were representative bodies at the prefectural level, promoting local self-government. A prefecture was different from the earlier daimyo domain. Political parties emerged in the 1880s. But the ministers were responsible to the emperor and not to the parliament. The emperor had many powers but they were exercised by officials.

Fukuzawa Yukichi (1835–1901) is called the father of modern Japan. He advocated educational reforms to emphasise practical knowledge and rational thinking and movement away from the earlier Confucian poetry-based curriculum. He was educated in the port cities of Nagasaki and Osaka, and these port cities had more Western influence. He was a part of the government fact-finding missions to the US in 1859 and 1862 and Europe in 1867. Fukuzawa Yukichi wrote the 10-volume work Conditions in the West, during the period between 1867 and 1870. In all, he wrote or translated more than 100 books on the US and Europe. He started a college in 1868, which later became a university. He did not take up any government position. He supported Japanese expansionism, saying that military force would prove more effective than diplomacy. But he died before Japan started expanding.

## *Japanese participation in World War II*

Japan always had a war-prone culture. They had the samurai tradition. They were a proud people, who gave importance to self-respect, honour and courage. They did not value life above everything, they were ready to kill and be killed for land or power or anything. This samurai spirit and fierce nationalism helped in increasing the pace of modernisation.

Japan was territorially a small country and did not have a base of natural resources. The people felt they needed to occupy more land to be powerful. They started the wars. In 1895 the war with China got Japan the Ryukyu islands and Taiwan. Traditionally, China was a great power and Japan was only a small island around China. But Japan modernised rapidly and took on China. This shocked the Chinese. Then the Russo-Japanese war took place in 1904-05 and Russia was defeated.

In 1910, Korea was annexed. During the 1920s and 1930s, the Japanese army became increasingly powerful. The army was answerable only to the emperor and not to the civilian government. In 1931, the Japanese army seized Manchuria. Japan disregarded the

League of Nations' disapproval of its invasion and got away with it without any penalty. This was one of the cases that exposed the weakness of the League of Nations. By 1932, the Japanese army was effectively in control of Manchuria. Japan then withdrew from the League of Nations.

In 1936, Japan joined Hitler-sponsored anti-Comintern pact. In the First World War, Japan was with the Allied Powers, not with the Central Powers. But in World War II, it sided with Hitler. Hitler was an inspiration to Japan.

In 1937, Japan invaded China, sending over one million soldiers there. The Japanese army committed innumerable atrocities in various parts of China. In one instance, in what came to be known as the Rape of Nanjing, the Japanese soldiers beheaded thousands of ordinary Chinese people, many other people were burnt alive, many infants were killed and some were even chopped to pieces, and the women were raped and not even older women were spared.

The point was to terrorise the civilians. If one city is terrorised like this, the other cities would not offer any resistance. It was the samurai approach applied in modern warfare. By 1939, Japan occupied a large portion of China.

By 1942, the Japanese power was at its peak. Japan occupied extensive territories in Southeast Asia. Japan even reached India. The Japanese army and the British army fought at Imphal. The Japanese wanted to take Australia at one end and India at another end.

Japan attacked Pearl Harbor in December 1941. This unprovoked act of aggression brought the US into the war. Because of the US participation in the war, it was very clear from 1943 onwards that Japan would lose. But the Japanese wouldn't surrender, nor would they treat surrendered people well. They killed many prisoners of war. To kill or to die – that seemed to be their ideology. On August 6, 1945, President Truman – who had taken over power recently after Roosevelt's death – ordered the dropping of atom bombs on Hiroshima and Nagasaki. The Second World War ended with that. The number of total casualties in this war was around 30 million.

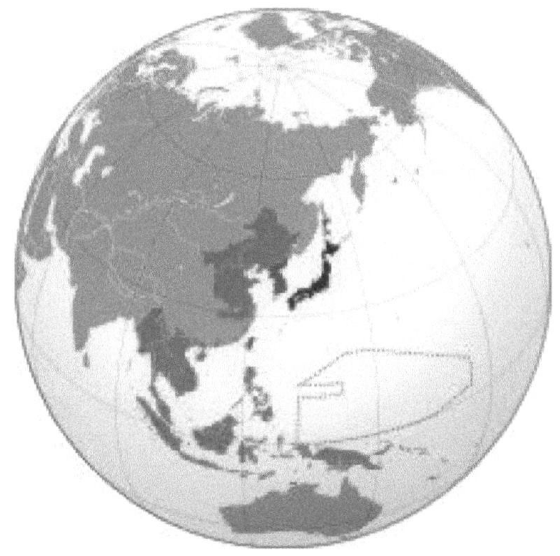

Japan by 1942

The Japanese general Hideki Tojo (1884–1948) was responsible for many of the country's war-related decisions. He was born in a samurai family. He was an army general for most of World War 2 and was also a minister of war in the cabinet. When the prime minister resigned in 1941 not liking the general's war plans, the general himself was appointed as the prime minister. Hideki Tojo advocated Japan's unprovoked attack on the US. He was responsible for the conquest of much of Southeast Asia. He was implicated in numerous war crimes and massacres of civilians, including the Rape of Nanjing. He was behind the ill-treatment of prisoners of war and the sexual enslavement of women. He promoted the idea that the Japanese were superior, and that they had the right to expand. In the end, after a failed attempt to commit suicide, he was arrested and was hanged as per the judgement of a tribunal, in 1948.

## *World War II*

Between 1939 and 1942, Germany and Japan were victorious. The Allied counter-attacks started in 1942. The Allied forces advanced in 1944 and 1945 and achieved final victory over Japan in August 1945, after the dropping of atom bombs. Germany had surrendered before.

Early on in the war, in 1940, Hitler struck France and it fell within six weeks. Churchill became the prime minister of Britain just before the fall of France. Churchill played a crucial role in turning the tide against Hitler. Hitler could not win the war against Britain also. Then he attacked Russia in June 1941, in Operation Barbarossa, which was a major mistake. Hitler's downfall began with it. Russia played a major role in defeating Germany. About 90% of all German soldiers were occupied on the Russian front, and about 80% of them were killed there.

Incidentally, there were many, including Mao, who warned Stalin that Hitler would invade Russia but Stalin did not believe that Hitler would do that. Why would Hitler do something so stupid, Stalin thought. Why did Hitler do it? He thought so highly of himself and thought that he could win Russia too and in a short time. One strategy in war is to attack someone when he is least prepared. Hitler thought that way. Similarly, Japan also thought someday the US would join the war anyway, and the US would not agree with Japan's imperialist ambitions – so why not attack the US before it gets ready?

Japan's attack on the US was a major miscalculation. The US might not have been able to respond immediately, but the US was a huge industrial power and an industrial power can be converted into military power in very little time. Hitler did not tell Japan that he was going to attack Russia, nor did Japan inform Hitler about its attack on Pearl Harbor. The end of Germany in the war was not far away now, and so was the end of Japan. The Allies concentrated on Germany first, and then they turned to the Pacific.

The Allies entered Berlin in May 1945, and Hitler committed suicide. Hitler had wanted his men either to fight or commit suicide. Fight all you can, and when you cannot anymore then commit suicide. It is said that Hitler was influenced by Nietzsche's philosophy. Nietzsche said things like you have to take up such a high mission in life that you would perish in achieving it. In trying to achieve world domination, Hitler perished. Hitler wanted the German people and soldiers too to have the same spirit.

Stalin also was against surrendering however desperate the situation may be. It was very clear to the Russian soldiers that they had to continue fighting under all circumstances, otherwise Stalin would kill them.

During the early phase of the war, the Jews used to be shot and buried in mass graves. But as Germany went on occupying more lands, it had to deal with many more Jews. Then Hitler thought of gas chambers. At the concentration camp in Auschwitz, a million people were killed in three years. There were gipsies and other people too among those who were killed. The average number of deaths at Auschwitz comes to 12,000 per day. It was like a factory to kill humans.

Italy was defeated in Ethiopia by Britain in 1941. In 1943, the king removed Mussolini from office and had him arrested. Mussolini was resigned to his fate, but Hitler rescued him and installed him as a ruler in the Nazi-occupied area of Italy. Hitler asked Mussolini to send the Jews in his region to the concentration camps and also execute his opponents who were responsible for his loss of power, which included members of his government and his son-in-law.

But Hitler was losing. Germany was pushed out of Italy. In 1945, Mussolini was executed by the people. The bodies of him and his mistress were battered, spit upon, and hung upside down. Hitler did not want to meet the same fate. Just 2 days after Mussolini was killed, Hitler and his mistress committed suicide and ordered their bodies to be burnt.

## *Japan after World War II*

In World War II, over two million Japanese died, the economy was ruined, and after the war, the country was temporarily occupied by America, under the supervision of General Douglas MacArthur. Japan then formed its government, which carried out many reforms.

The parliament, known as Diet, became important. The emperor who was all-powerful earlier now remained only as a symbol. Japan forever renounced war "as a sovereign right of the nation." It would be having only a small army, but the country was protected by the US. The top war leaders of World War II were prosecuted. Some land reforms, as well as tax reforms, were introduced. The effort was to create a more egalitarian society.

Though America bombed Japan during World War II, and the Japanese government was under American supervision, Japan carried out all these reforms. After such a desperate, energetic fight during the war, the Japanese decided to forever renounce the war. They accepted an alliance with the US and the US nuclear umbrella was extended. In return, the US was to have military bases there. Shigeru Yoshida who was the Japanese prime minister during 1946-47 and 1948-54 adopted what later came to be called the Yoshida Doctrine. By this policy, military spending was confined only to 1% of the GDP, and more importance was given to the economy and trade.

Interestingly, though the US pressured Japan to spend more on the military, Japan refused to do so. Japan saw huge economic progress because of a high saving rate, highly educated and disciplined workforce, government-supported business, and focus on technology. There was a 10% annual GDP growth between 1950 and 1975, in Japan. By 1985, Japan was second in GDP in the world, though the country is geographically so small. China on the other hand started growing only many years later.

Being a small country, Japan did not have many raw materials and sources of energy. Nevertheless, it adapted to its limitations and went on rising, with the help of high technology. The higher level of technological sophistication in Japanese society could happen because of a highly educated population.

At one time Japan had been a very isolated country, and then it was modernised, it wanted to be like a European country, and it indeed became like that, waging an aggressive war in World War II. After the war, the country completely changed. It understood that the focus should be not on the military but rather on the economy.

From the '90s on, its economic growth slowed down. The annual GDP growth rate was only 1.3% between 1990 and 2002. People said Japan was declining. But in what sense was it declining? Not by any objective criteria of what makes a good life. The Japanese were healthy, educated, living long and wealthy. The GDP grew so high up to 1990 that the growth naturally became less from then. Moreover, as the country developed, its population growth rate went down and people were living longer. As the ratio of the elderly increased, economic growth kept decreasing.Japan is now the third largest economy in the world, with China being the second. Many think Japan should continue to grow. Japan adopted many policies other countries adopt in such a situation, but it was not able to increase growth. Coming to fiscal policies, the government spent much, but this only made the country get into debt trouble. Coming to monetary policies, it gave a negative interest rate! But these policies did not make much difference. Perhaps Japan has reached what can be reached, given the economic tools that books suggest. Perhaps Japan has nobody to follow now, nor does it have anybody to advise it.

## *Think on it*

1. What was a shogunate?
2. Who was a daimyo?
3. Who were the samurai?
4. What was the importance of Tokugawa shogunate?
5. What changes did the Meiji Revolution bring in Japan?

6. Why is Fukuzawa Yukichi called the father of modern Japan?
7. What wars did Japan win before 1937?
8. What areas did Japan occupy by 1942?
9. How did World War 2 end in the Pacific theatre?
10. What do you know about Hideki Tojo?
11. What happened to the Jews in the territories occupied by Germany?
12. Trace the events that led to the execution of Mussolini.
13. Trace the events that led to the suicide of Hitler.
14. What is Yoshida Doctrine? Why did Japan adopt it?

CHAPTER TEN

# Decolonisation

Colonisation took place at one time, and after some years the colonised countries were getting independent, that is called decolonisation. We are looking at decolonisation in the context of Asia, Africa, and Latin America. What is the historic significance of decolonisation?

Was colonisation a bad development? History textbooks usually tell that colonisation was bad, the natives were exploited, eventually, they understood it and fought for freedom and finally, they became free. So independence is a good thing and colonisation was like enslavement. But I don't think that is the way history should be taught. Colonisation led to the spread of modernisation.

It is taught that colonialism exploited people. But if that was true, the non-colonised countries across the world must be doing better than the colonised countries. That does not seem to be the case though. We can also see it in the context of India's states. The first colonised province was Bengal, and it was much better off than other provinces by the time of Independence. Coastal Andhra was completely colonised while Telangana was a princely state, and coastal Andhra was much better off.

Colonisation was the path to modernisation. The colonisers wanted to extract surplus from the people or the land, but they could do so only by developing the resources, and by training the men. That was how the middle classes emerged in India.

It was from a Western perspective that these educated people in India looked at their society, and they wanted to change it. When they thought they were capable of self-governing, they wanted the British to get out. All of this was an educational process. Colonisation was one stage in history, and decolonisation was another stage. One cannot say that colonisation was something bad and only decolonisation was good.

India became a nation only after colonisation, many other countries too became nations only after colonisation. The nationalism that developed in Europe first spread all over the world during colonisation. Otherwise, the identities of people in countries like India had been based on tribe, caste, religion, race etc.

How would it have been if there was no colonisation? It is not that if these colonised countries had not been colonised, they would have developed and become stronger on their own. They would have remained weak and backward most probably. They would have been attacked by stronger countries later.

Conquest contributes to cultural change. Why should culture spread this way, couldn't it spread peacefully? If people from Britain came here and engaged in the discussion of Vedas and Upanishads, would the Indians have listened? Not very likely. Instead, when they were defeated and ruled, when their tradition was ridiculed, then they started listening. What were the socio-religious reform movements in India? They were an outcome of loss of power, and because of loss of power, some Indians started thinking: what are we up to?

## *Decolonisation*

By the end of World War II, many European countries became weak and exhausted, they did not have sufficient motivation to continue with colonialism. Many people from the colonial countries took part in the war and understood how the Europeans are like any other human beings and not superior. Meanwhile, a new ideology was also spreading all over the world, the ideology of freedom.

Between 1946 and 1974, most colonised countries became independent. In August 1941, the US and Britain released what is called the Atlantic Charter on the post-war world. They said that no country would expand after the war. If a country wins a particular territory, it is not going to possess that. Self-determination became an accepted principle after the Atlantic Charter.

The US and Britain were positioned differently on the issue of decolonisation. Britain had a huge empire and the US did not, it only had the Philippines. The US was not for the continuation of colonialism. The US came to be seen as a friend by many leaders of the colonised countries. The formation of the UN was also being discussed around that time, and the UN also was for anti-colonialism and self-determination.

More and more people got to see the real nature of colonialism as economic exploitation. In India, the extremists said that the real purpose of colonialism was economic exploitation, while the moderates took a more positive view of it.

Some countries such as India, Vietnam, and the Philippines got independence through struggle. French-speaking Western Africa, Libya, Iraq and some more got their independence as a sudden offer because the European powers simply did not want to rule anymore, they were too exhausted.

Britain gave freedom to India, Sri Lanka and Myanmar in the late 1940s and to other countries later. Belgians, Dutch and Portuguese were all forced out of the countries they colonised or faced international pressure to do so.

## *Vietnam conflict*

Vietnam is a more recent case of decolonisation. The Vietnam conflict reflects many aspects of the post-World War 2 world such as nationalism, communism, and the Cold War. Vietnam is also remembered as a case where America failed despite trying its best to resolve the conflict to its advantage. When America was invading Afghanistan, some thought the American soldiers would undo the bad memory of what happened in Vietnam. However, the Vietnam experience was only repeated in Afghanistan. About 57,000 Americans were killed in the Vietnam conflict, and one trillion dollars were spent. Hundreds of thousands of Vietnamese died.

Why was America involved in the Vietnam conflict? Vietnam was a French colony, but during World War II Japan came to occupy Vietnam. During the time of Japanese occupation, in 1941, the Vietnamese leader Ho Chi Minh returned from Europe to fight against Japan. The US under the leadership of Roosevelt cooperated with Vietnam in its fight against Japan.

Japan lost the Second World War. Then there was a fight between the French and the Vietnamese. After the Japanese left, the French regained their control of Vietnam, but now the US took the French side, under Truman's presidency. This was happening in the 1950s when the Cold War was escalating.

It was the US and French versus the Vietnamese. Ho Chi Minh's organisation, Vietminh, defeated the French in 1954. After that, a conference was held in Geneva and an agreement was made to partition Vietnam into north and south, with the north ruled by Ho Chi Minh. The South Vietnamese government, which was very corrupt and unpopular, was supported by the US, under Eisenhower's administration.

The fight for freedom continued in South Vietnam under the leadership of the National Liberation Front, FLN in French. North Vietnam, under Ho's control, and South Vietnam fought each other. China, by then a communist country, joined the side of the North. And South Vietnam became a theatre for an ideological battle for America, it did not want to lose South Vietnam, so it started spending more and more money and was sending more and more troops. Even the American ground troops were committed to the war in Vietnam in 1965. Nixon came to power in 1968, and by then half a million US ground troops were engaged in Vietnam. But still, the Americans were nowhere near victory.

The US withdrew its troops in 1973, asking the South Vietnamese government to defend itself. That government was very weak. In 1975, North Vietnamese troops took over South Vietnam. The US helicopters lifted the last Americans from the US embassy in South Vietnam. It was the same situation during the recent American evacuation of Afghanistan.

Historians think that America misjudged the situation in Vietnam. America underestimated the power of nationalism, it simply saw the situation through the lens of the Cold War. The US might have been a better political and economic system, but if it wanted to impose it on a people against their will, they could make it a fight for their independence. Finally, a united Vietnam was created under the leadership of Ho Chih Minh.

Soon after America left Vietnam, there was a war between Vietnam and China, though both of them were communists, and later there was a war between China and USSR, again both communists. This shows that nationalism is a more important force than ideological similarity.

## *Africa colonised*

Colonisation in Africa was a very sudden process. Up to 1880, Africa was called the 'Informal Empire' of the European powers. Why so? Certain European countries went to Africa mainly for gold, and very soon they found that Africa had something even more lucrative to offer, which was the men themselves, as slaves. The Europeans formed certain trading posts around the coastal belt of Africa, and the most important thing they were doing was the slave trade. They were not going into the interior, because in the interior of Africa there were many problems such as malaria and all kinds of diseases.

Why did the slave trade start in Africa? Plantations that began in other places such as America brought demand for cheap labour. Many native American tribes got extinct by that time in both North and South America. The countries in North and South America then had a demand for cheap labour from Africa.

But don't think that the Europeans introduced slavery in Africa. Slavery had already been there for centuries. Who would become slaves? If one group invaded another and defeated it, men from the defeated group would be taken as slaves by the invaders. Slavery was there even in Socrates' times in Greece, it was an age-old institution, and it was there in Africa too. But slave trade on such a long distance, called the Atlantic trade, happened only because of the European powers.

This tradition of slavery was changed by colonialism. The Portuguese or other European powers would come to Africa, they would want to buy slaves. Who would give them? It was the Africans only. And how would they get thc slaves? They would conduct raids on other groups, turn some people into slaves and sell them. Because of the demand for human labour across the Atlantic, much disturbance was being created in Africa, with more and more raids happening. To speed up this process of enslavement of the people, the Europeans brought weapons and technology to Africa.

Traditionally, slavery in Africa was limited in scale and was also not so inhuman. The slaves were sometimes accepted as family members and sometimes they were also freed, because after all it was one African enslaving another African, and the one who is slaving himself could have been enslaved under different circumstances.

Between 1650 and 1870, an estimated 40 million slaves travelled across the Atlantic. Sometimes people died on the way because they were put in many unhygienic conditions. Sometimes there were slave revolts. Though they were chained, they offered a lot of resistance. Still, they were taken and put to work. Some Africans cooperated with the Europeans to enslave other Africans. Internal rivalries within the African society became a resource for the European slave trade.

Opposition to the slave trade began in Europe first. Some people in these countries raised moral questions regarding the slave trade. Britain abolished the slave trade in 1807 and the US in 1808. Other European countries followed soon, because of the anti-slavery movement in these countries. The anti-slavery movement was a humanistic movement and a good thing, but some economic reasons also played a role in abolishing the slave trade. The Industrial Revolution demanded Africa to be used as a source of raw materials and as a market for finished products. They wanted to make African countries the same as they made other colonised countries elsewhere. Then started a scramble for Africa and the resources it could provide.

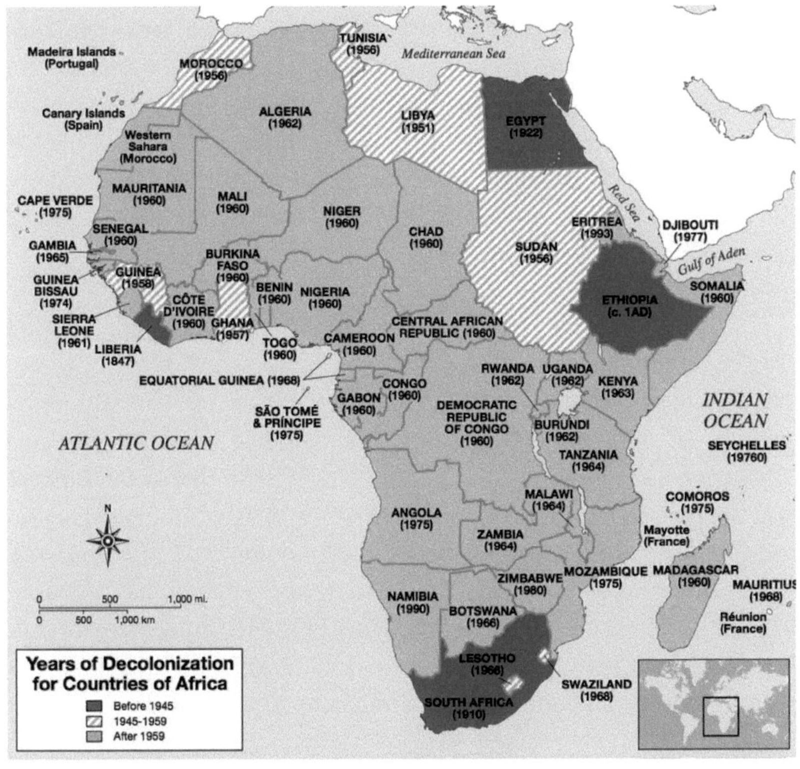


Africa decolonized

Colonisation started rather suddenly. Before 1880, only Algeria and South Africa were under direct European control. By 1914, only Ethiopia and Liberia remained outside European control.

Between 1880 and World War I, most of Africa got colonised.

The way the Europeans colonised some of these African countries was that they would provide proof that they had some contacts, some administration there, and they would claim the land. That was how the European powers divided the entire continent of Africa among themselves. Britain got a very big share, starting from south to north.

Racism developed as a result of slavery. When there was slavery going on in Africa, there was nothing like racism, as all the people were blacks. But when the black people were made to work as slaves in the Americas, the white people needed a justification for the enslavement. How could they do to the African people what they would not do to their people? Then came the idea that black people were inferior. The existence of two races with two completely different social and economic positions side by side gave rise to racism.

## *Africa decolonised*

The process of decolonisation in Africa also happened suddenly. Around 35 African countries got decolonised between 1950 to 1965. Decolonisation in Africa was related to the changes in Europe and the overall ideology that was reshaping the world. In Africa too, there were nationalist movements and in some African countries, nationalism moved from elitism to mass movements. It was elitist in many African countries before World War II, but there emerged new leaders then. Like in India, the elites in African countries were impacted and shaped by colonialism, even as these countries benefitted from colonialism.

There is one difference between India and some countries in Africa. In the case of India, the British did not come here to settle. India was not a settlers' colony. The British officers would come to India to work as administrators and would go back after retirement. In some African countries, the rulers did not go back to Europe. In such cases, independence became more difficult. For example,

South Africa became free for the native black people only in 1994.

Why was there apartheid only in South Africa and not in other African countries? Apartheid arose in South Africa not only because of racial differences but also because of the lucrative trade in diamonds. The whites did not want any competition from the black people. At the same time, they wanted black labour at a very cheap price. They had to discriminate against the black people, they had to segregate and control them. They had to show the black people how inferior they were. If someone was working in a diamond mine, he would be searched very thoroughly while leaving work. In that context, some extreme forms of discrimination emerged.

Africa provides an extreme case of the problems of colonisation as well as decolonisation. When the European powers were dividing Africa among themselves, they did it randomly without attention to the people. We can see the borders of many African countries as straight lines. How can a border be a straight line? A part of a tribe could be on one side and another part of the tribe could be on the other side.

Many countries in Africa are too artificial creations. People of an African country might not have had any collective experience. Many of the groups belonging to a country may be traditional rivals to one another. There could be ethnic conflicts. When the colonial powers were ruling these African countries, they imposed what's known as the Westminster model on them. What's this model? You have a prime minister or a president, you have just one person to control the entire territory. If a single person who comes from a particular tribe and region is controlling the entire territory, why would people of other tribes and regions want to obey him?

All the people of a nation are expected to elect one person and that person is supposed to provide an impartial rule to everybody, according to the political model. But this was not a part of the African ethos. An alien political and administrative structure was imposed on Africa. This was also the case with other colonised countries but to a lesser extent than in Africa. In India also, disparate cultural groups were brought together under one nation.

This kind of forced living together would not lead to stable political entities. It might result in warfare across groups. A person with superior military power may become a dictator. Some African countries also got involved in the Cold War. If a president was supporting one superpower, rival groups would get support from another superpower, which would worsen the existing divisions.

## *Latin America*

Why is South America also called Latin America? Because it was ruled by Spain and Portugal. The languages of Spanish, Portuguese and French were developed from Latin, the ancient language of Rome. Most South American countries were ruled by Spain, the remaining countries were ruled by Portugal and others. The Latin American colonisation and decolonisation experiences were different compared to the African and Asian experiences. The Latin American decolonisation experience was closer to the US decolonisation experience.

What was the US decolonisation experience? We call it the American War of Independence. Thinking in terms of decolonisation, America was decolonised from whom? It was from Britain. It was the British people only who went to America and settled there. And Britain had control over America. In time, the people staying in America declared independence against those ruling from Britain. Both were the same English people. This was unlike India's case.

The English in America revolted against the English in Britain. Latin American countries too were like that. Many of those countries were under the occupation of Spain, some were under Portugal. Spain and Portugal were not so powerful countries. Napoleon invaded Spain and Portugal in 1808 and defeated them. The defeat of Spain and Portugal in Europe set the movements of independence in the Latin American countries in motion. The councils in these countries declared new governments and banished the viceroys, a viceroy being the representative of the ruling power.

In Latin America, people who were whole of Spanish descent but born in the New World were called criollos, 'the New World' being another term for the Americas. These criollos were eager to take power away from the peninsulars, that is, the people from Europe. Like the English in America trying to get independence from the English in Britain, the criollos here were doing the same with the peninsulars. How about the natives? The natives were in a much inferior position socially and economically. Criollos vs peninsulars was a fight between the elites, Latin American and European elites.

Wars of independence took place in many countries between 1810 and 1825. Except in Haiti, these revolts were led by conservative and wealthy men. The elites who won independence for their countries did not try to put a democratic arrangement in place. It was much later that the middle classes emerged. They started demanding more power and more say in the decision-making structures, because of which certain changes started taking place.

When Spain and Portugal became powerful again, did they try to control Latin American countries? They did not, because, by 1823, the US president James Monroe declared what came to be called Monroe Doctrine, according to which European powers could not interfere in the affairs of Latin American countries. The US made the Monroe Doctrine the core of its foreign policy, it said that the Americas are its sphere of influence and Europe cannot interfere. Much later it did not allow the USSR's influence also. The US did many things in Latin American countries, first to control and contain the European influence and later the communist influence.

## *Think on it*

1. What is meant by decolonisation?

2. What are the positive things about colonisation?
3. How did WW II contribute to decolonisation?
4. How did Vietnam become independent?
5. How was the US involved in the Vietnam conflict?
6. What is meant by Africa being Europe's informal empire?
7. Why did slave trade start in Africa?
8. How did slavery lead to racism?
9. What is a settlers' colony?
10. Why did apartheid develop in South Africa?
11. Why are Western political institutions less suitable to Africa?
12. How is decolonisation in Latin America different from that in Asia and Africa?
13. What is the significance of the Monroe Doctrine?

CHAPTER ELEVEN

# The Chinese Revolution

It may be easier to understand the history of China by comparing it with that of India. India was divided into many kingdoms, then the British came, they defeated most of them, and created one India. Then they also educated some people and helped in modernising the country. An educated elite emerged in the nineteenth century, and these people wanted the country to be free. There was the freedom struggle. In time, the British left. In China's case, although it was colonised by Western powers, it was not colonised by any one country, and therefore it was not unified by any colonial power. It was also not modernised by any of the colonial powers.

During the era of colonisation, many Western powers occupied various parts of China. The British had control of one region, the French of another, and the Russians and Germans had their regions. Besides these Western powers, the Japanese too came to occupy a part of China. Although China remained divided, there was a cultural unity and a continuity of civilization.

When colonisation began, the Chinese rulers were weak. As in India, the British began with trade in China and started taking over territories. The opium wars that took place from 1839 to 42 between Britain and China show how it was happening. At first, the British East India Company was buying tea, silks and other goods from China, paying in gold and silver, but when the company did not have enough gold and silver, it started bartering opium obtained from India.

The Chinese rulers, however, did not want opium in their country because it would lead to addiction. They started restricting the supply of opium, which the British did not like. Then the British and the Chinese fought over this issue, China lost and was forced to sign treaties ceding some territories to Britain. China had to make similar treaties with the US, France and Germany.

In the case of India, the British power became like India's power. No such thing in the case of China. China went on to become weaker throughout the nineteenth century.

## *Sun Yat-sen*

Sun Yat-sen (1866–1925) is called the father of modern China. He was born in a peasant family but benefited from Western education in a Christian school in Hawaii. He was influenced by Lincoln's definition of democracy: "of the people, by the people and for the people." Later he wrote a book on democracy Three Principles of the People. Sun wanted to establish a democratic and modern China. He attempted a coup in 1895 but it failed. He began impacting people through his writings and speeches. In 1911, the Qing monarchy was overthrown by the military. Sun had no direct involvement in the coup, but because people had respect for him, he was made the pro-term president of the new republic of China, created in 1912. But General Yuan Shikai soon replaced Sun.

Yuan Shikai wanted to be like a king himself and did not respect the institutions of democracy, but he died within a few years, in 1916. Now there was anarchy in the country, and warlords in different parts of China, supported by foreign powers, were fighting among themselves. Sun wanted to end this anarchy. He set up an institution for military training. He also founded the Kuomintang or the Nationalist Party. Sun Yat-sen's commandant Chiang Kai-shek played an important role in defeating the warlords. He created a unified China by 1926.

The Marxist ideas and the Russian Revolution were an inspiration to some people in China, who formed the Communist Party of China in 1921. Sun had a liking for the communists, he found that they were more energetic and people-oriented. Sun's thinking was also closer to communist thinking. He believed in a strong state. He said that a nation should have unlimited freedom, but an individual should have limited freedom. He was also keen on promoting the welfare of workers and peasants. He allowed the communists to be a part of the Nationalist Party and was happy with some changes they brought in the party.

Sun Yat-sen's attitude towards the communists was not liked by many other party members. They feared that if the communists were allowed into the party, they would take over the party. They considered the communists to be their real enemies. These people preferred American cooperation, whereas the communists preferred Russian cooperation. The party's main base was the middle class and the landlords, whereas the communists were more favourable to the peasants, the workers and the lower classes. Under Sun Yat-sen's leadership, however, the communists worked closely with the nationalists and played a role in the unification of the country.

## *Rise of Mao*

It was Mao Zedong ( 1893-1976) who made China take the path of communism. Marx said that the industrial workers would bring communism, but Mao realised that in China peasants should play an important role. Mao and his associates were good at guerrilla warfare. They also promoted a strong sense of Chinese nationalism.

Mao Zedong

The Long March of 1934 was an important event in the history of modern China. The communists were being persecuted by the Nationalists by this time. To protect themselves, the communists wanted to take refuge in a faraway place. They walked over 6000 miles in one year and moved to Shensi near the Mongolian border. They managed to barricade themselves there. But out of 100,000 peasants who started the march, only 10,000 survived. Mao now became the undisputed leader of the communists. Before that, the Russian advisors were being given importance.

Japan occupied Manchuria, a territory in northeast China, in 1931. The army commander there simply surrendered. The Japanese then invaded all of China in 1937, but the Chinese resisted. A lot of fighting followed. Two major cities, Beijing and Nanjing, fell into the Japanese hands. Much of coastal China came under Japan's control. The year 1937 is regarded as the beginning of World War II in Asia.

The Japanese invasion brought both the rival political parties in China together. But the Chiang government was not actively fighting the Japanese, whereas the communists were giving them a tough fight. When Japan occupied some areas, the Nationalist government moved towards the west, and many people moved along with it. Some of these people moved into an area which was occupied by the communists, called Yenan. Here, military and ideological training was given to them by the communists. As more people joined the communists during the war years, their numbers grew to one million.

The Communist Party became so popular that it set up branches in every village, there were different wings for women and youth, and one exclusively for educators. The Nationalists were unpopular in the areas they were present and ineffective against the Japanese. The conscripts they got were not motivated enough to fight the Japanese, and Chiang himself thought that Japan would leave one day but the communists were the main threat. He told a reporter once that Japan is a disease of the skin, whereas communism is a disease of the heart. America was giving money and weaponry to the Nationalist government, but the government was not doing much in fighting the Japanese. The Second World War ended in 1945, by which time the communists in China became more powerful, more popular and occupied more areas than the Nationalists.

The civil war between the communists and the Nationalists took place from 1946 to 1949. The Americans tried to mediate between the two but failed. They didn't want to lose China to Russia, but it happened anyway. Big cities fell into communist hands in 1948. By October 1949, the communists were all over China. The Nationalists fled to Taiwan. There they said that one day they would get back to mainland China, though it never happened.

## *Mao's China*

Mao followed Leninism in things like land redistribution, collectivisation and industrialisation, except that he gave more role to the peasantry in the revolution. There was only one party and no free media. It was a party dictatorship. There was no separation of powers between the legislature, executive and judiciary.

There was violence during the land redistribution phase. The redistribution was not based on any proper surveying, recording and transparent implementation of the land ceiling. The communist party cadres would go to a village and they would declare somebody as a class enemy, they would declare his supporters as class enemies, and they would all be persecuted. Sometimes someone in the party may be the son of a landlord who is declared a class enemy. Mao realised that these divisions could be a barrier to the mobilisation of the people and so he discontinued land redistribution during the war against the Japanese and the civil war.

Then came collectivisation which meant people living and working in communes. Some of the communes were very big, consisting of 25,000 people. All the farmers had to work according to a strict discipline imposed by the party. And they could take only part of their produce for their personal use. Everything had to be cooked in the communal kitchen only. If there was any transgression or resistance to the program, the people were punished, and sometimes entire villages were punished. The whole population was thus reduced to bonded labour. Collectivisation took place between 1955 and 57.

Millions of people were imprisoned or killed or died in other ways during Mao's regime. There were huge famines brought about by human doing. At one time when the grain production was low, Mao saw some sparrows eating grains. All sparrows in the land were then ordered to be killed. People would make a lot of noise so that the sparrows couldn't rest anywhere and they would get exhausted and fall down and then the people would kill them. But when the sparrows died, there were locust attacks. Mao had no understanding of how the ecological cycle works. A politician should seek the advice of the experts in such matters, but someone like Mao never did that.

During the famines, people were subjected to extreme suffering. There were instances of people eating white porcelain-colored mud.

Recently a Hong Kong University professor Frank Dikotter made an extensive study of Mao's regime, based on newly opened archives, and wrote three books, "Mao's Great Famine: The History of China's Most Devastating Catastrophe, 1958–62," "The Tragedy of Liberation: A History of the Chinese Revolution, 1945–1957" and "The Cultural Revolution: A People's History, 1962–1976." Around 45 million Chinese people died from starvation during the famines. In all, more than 65 million people died during Mao's regime, according to the Black Book of Communism. To put it in perspective, 65 million is more than the total number of casualties in World War I and World War II put together.

In 1958, Mao started a movement he called the Great Leap Forward, introducing mass industrialisation. The communes were now given the task of producing steel. It was called "backyard steel-making." Untrained people were trying to do many things, it turned out to be a costly failure that led the economy into a depression.

When so many failures were taking place, instead of accepting his role in them, Mao called for the Great Proletarian Cultural Revolution in 1965. Frank Dikotter says that whereas Lenin and Stalin declared only some classes of people as enemies, Mao thought the Chinese culture itself was the enemy. Mao thought communism would be successful when the culture itself was changed.

Books, artworks, and musical records were all destroyed. Going beyond things related to tradition and culture, Mao's people attacked writers, artists, intellectuals, professors and doctors. Doctors were asked to scrub the hospital floors, professors were made to wear dunce caps, walk on all fours and bark like dogs, many were sent to villages, and some were killed. Groups of Red Guards, mainly consisting of students, were asked to make war on the older generations. The students would memorise what was called the red little book, titled Thoughts of Chairman Mao. They would shout slogans, criticise people, and commit acts of violence. In this process, many people who were considered to be Mao's opponents were eliminated. So much chaos was created that the country fell into anarchy. The army had to intervene in 1969 to restore some order.

In 1967, Liu Shaoqui, who was second in command in the Communist Party, was imprisoned, regularly beaten and called things like "renegade, traitor, scab." He died in prison. This happened to the No. 2 himself, so we can imagine the fate of many others within the party and outside. It was much later that Deng Xiaoping restored Liu's name and honour. By the 1980s, the Cultural Revolution was condemned and Mao's portraits were silently removed from public places.

From 1971 onwards and even before, many people understood clearly that Maoism was a colossal failure. By the 1970s, there was emerging capitalism in China, many Chinese were involved in the informal market, bribing the bureaucracy when needed. Deng who ruled China from the late 70s is usually credited with bringing capitalism to China, but Dikotter says it was not really Deng who brought the market reforms but the people.

Maoism was a disaster and it ruined China. One would think that a man like Mao would be cursed and despised, but he is still adored to this day in China. Why does he still have some statues in China? It is because the same communist party is ruling. They are not in a position to denounce him because then their own legitimacy could be questioned. Besides, there is the fact that Mao freed China from foreign powers and unified the country, and that is still something that people respect him for.

## *Deng's Reforms*

Deng Xiaoping

Mao died in 1976. During the last years of Mao's life, he was not of sound mind, he couldn't comprehend the situation, others were leading the country on his behalf, and his wife played a very important role in it. A clique called the Gang of Four, which included Mao's wife, Jiang Qing, and her associates committed many atrocities, along with general Lin Biao. In the end, all of them were put on trial, and the power came to Deng Xiaoping. He led the country till his death in 1997, trying to undo the damage done by Mao. He had been a prisoner during Mao's Cultural Revolution.

While China was still ruled by the communist party, Deng Xiaoping introduced a free market economy to China, along with the right for farmers to cultivate some land. It was Deng's reforms that led to huge economic growth in the country. The GDP growth rate of China between 1984 and 2008 was 9 per cent. Communism had wreaked havoc on Chinese society, but capitalism made it powerful just within a few decades. However, capitalism in China was not Western-type capitalism, it was and still is under communist political control, with state-led enterprises playing a major role in the economic growth.

The relations between China and the USA also changed over the decades. Nixon visited China in 1972. China became a member of the WTO in 2001. In the early 90s, China opened up its economy for free trade and the influx of foreign capital. China's worry during these years was that it should not go through what the USSR went through.Some people think that the government's role with a commitment to economic growth made the enormous success possible and if China had a free-market form of capitalism like anywhere else it wouldn't have been as successful. That is one argument.

## *Think on it*

1. What was the political situation in China before it became unified?
2. What do you know about the opium wars between Britain and China?
3. Who was Sun Yat-sen?
4. Who was Chiang Kai-shek?
5. What was Kuomintang or the Nationalist Party?
6. What do you know about the Long March of 1934?
7. How did the communists become more popular during the war with Japan?
8. What were the elements of Leninism that Mao followed?
9. What was Mao's Great Leap Forward?
10. Why did Mao start the Cultural Revolution?
11. Was Maoism a great failure? Explain.
12. What do you know about the context and the nature of Deng's reforms in China?

CHAPTER TWELVE

# Cold War

The Cold War was a situation of protracted conflict between the US and USSR, though there was no actual war between them. Hence it is called Cold War. Certain developments after World War II resulted in this Cold War that lasted for the next few decades.

Why didn't it turn hot? It was for a very simple reason as both the countries had nuclear weapons by the 50s. We don't know how things would have been if not for these weapons of mass destruction. Full-fledged wars between great powers became impossible after the advent of nuclear weapons.

## *Creation of the Soviet bloc*

For a long time, Britain had a huge empire and it was the most powerful country on earth. But by the end of World War II, the US became more powerful because Britain was losing colonies and was exhausted by the war. The USSR did not have any colonies, but it consisted of many countries and also had many satellite countries and it was a huge empire.

How did the USSR get its satellite countries? Towards the end of the Second World War, the Soviet forces entered Germany from the east and arrived in Berlin. The American and British forces arrived from the west, and Berlin fell. The WW II was over. Once the war was over and Germany has surrendered, all the Allied forces, including the Soviets, should have gone back. But that did not happen. The Soviet forces were stationed in the middle of

Berlin and the American and British forces agreed that the USSR could have control over all those areas it crossed in its long march to Berlin.

Of the total 50 million dead in World War II, half of them civilians, 20 million were from the USSR. It played a crucial role in defeating Hitler, but does it mean that the world should agree that all the areas through which the Soviet army marched now belonged to the USSR? That meant that one was handing over these countries in Eastern Europe from the Nazis to the Soviets. Unfortunately, that was what happened as a result of the conferences between the Allies.

The Yalta conference took place in February 1945 between Britain, the US and the USSR as represented by Churchill, Roosevelt and Stalin respectively. Yalta was in the USSR. Later in the same year, one more conference was held in Potsdam, Germany, between July 17 and August 2. But by this time Roosevelt died, and was replaced by Truman. Elections were held in Britain, Churchill lost and Atlee became the prime minister. The beginning part of this conference was represented by Churchill and the later part by Atlee. The result of these conferences was that the USSR would have control over those areas it crossed but it was expected to hold free elections in those countries. However, it would have been obvious to everyone that the USSR would not hold free elections and would simply occupy these countries.

Unlike in the case of the Treaty of Versailles after the First World War, the Yalta and Potsdam summits were not critically looked at in the standard textbooks. I think these conferences should be regarded as great blunders. Only in the more recent years, in 2005, did US president George W Bush compare the Yalta conference to Chamberlain's concessions to Hitler in Munich in 1938, which were called appeasement. Bush called the Yalta conference "one of the greatest wrongs of history." However, Churchill very well knew then itself that this was gravely wrong. He wrote to his wife at this time, "The misery of the whole world appals me and I fear increasingly that new struggles may arise out of those we are successfully ending." Churchill clearly understood the repercussions of handing over huge territories of Eastern Europe to Stalin.

What did Stalin think? He said, "Everyone imposes his own system as far his army can reach." Stalin thought, we came this far, so all the territory up to here is ours. Stalin simply wanted to impose his system by force on all the countries of Eastern Europe.

## *Western Europe*

The United States helped restore the devastated countries of Western Europe after the Second World War. It helped promote democracy in these countries. Then it extended great economic help under what was called the Marshall Plan. In time, the countries of Western Europe were integrated, there was an economic union. They became prosperous. These countries became closer to the US. The economic assistance increased trade and interdependence between Europe and the US. The US itself was becoming powerful by promoting freedom and prosperity in other countries.

In 1944, even before the Second World War ended, IMF and World Bank were set up as a result of a conference at Bretton Woods. This conference was held because the US and countries of Western Europe were trying to see how to avoid the situation that many countries faced after World War I. Also, they learned certain lessons during the Great Depression earlier. They believed that several countries should be helped and some international coordination was needed, so they thought of IMF and World Bank. The GATT, which was about trade, came about in 1947.

In 1947 the US announced the Marshall Plan, named after the US secretary of state, for the reconstruction of Europe. It was a more direct effort to rebuild the shattered economies of Europe. While Stalin was busy taking the industrial equipment from East Germany, the US was helping Western Europe develop. In 1951, the European Coal and Steel Authority was established. In the subsequent decades, there would be increasing integration of the countries of Western Europe.

In 1947 came the Truman Doctrine – a policy to support free people anywhere in the world. The Truman Doctrine came after Eastern Europe was taken over by Stalin. The American president now said that he would defend the free world.

## *Eastern Europe*

In 1949, the Soviets successfully tested their atomic bomb. Then in 1955, the Warsaw Pact was formed, opposing the US-led alliance NATO that was formed in 1949.

What did Stalin do in the areas where he had control? He implemented what was called 'Sovietisation' or 'communisation'. Let's look at the economic dimensions of this process. The land properties in these countries of Eastern Europe were first redistributed and then collectivised. Then there was rapid industrialisation of these countries with a focus on heavy industry. Why heavy industry? Because they wanted to develop the infrastructure for the future, while the needs of present consumption were ignored. Politically, these countries had no freedom. A one party rule was imposed on these countries, and there was a strong secret police.

The methods Stalin used in imposing his political system on the countries of Eastern Europe were not different from the methods Hitler used to come to power. First, the communists get some supporters and they may form a party. Then they eliminate some of their opponents. Finally, all other political parties are thrown out. Or the communists may form a coalition with other parties, but they finally become one party with the elimination of the inconvenient people in the coalition. Sometimes, the small communist party will merge with a popular party and then start controlling it. Coercion, propaganda and all kinds of tricks were used in a variety of ways to capture political power.

These satellite countries could not have an independent foreign policy. The countries of the Warsaw Pact could not choose to be a part of the Marshall Plan. They could have no contact with international institutions, no trade with Western Europe.

## *Germany*

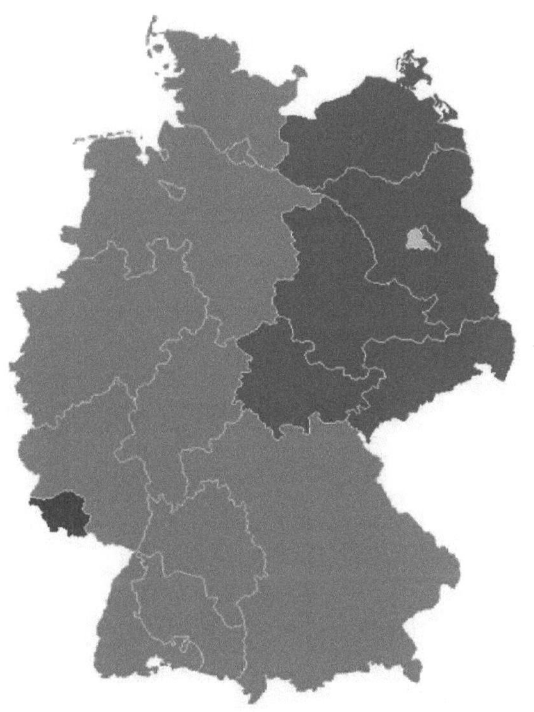

Germany divided

As a result of the Yalta and Potsdam conferences, parts of Germany were handed over to the Allied armies. Germany's eastern border moved a hundred miles west, and East Germany was taken by the USSR. There were originally British and American zones and they merged in 1947; in May 1949, West Germany was formed out of three zones given to the US, Britain and France. Germany was thus split into two parts, with East Germany developing in one way and West Germany in another way.

The German capital Berlin was very much within East Germany, and the city itself was divided, first into four and after that into two. In June 1948, in what came to be known as the Berlin blockade, Stalin blocked ground access to West Berlin. The essential supplies to the city had to be airlifted for 11 months.

## *Poland*

Border changes of Poland

As a result of the war, Poland's borders changed. It lost a huge area of land to Russia but gained a part of Germany. In 1939, at the inception of the Second World War, Germany invaded Poland. Later, the Soviets invaded Poland from the east. Hitler and Stalin agreed and, they divided Poland between them. Germany began the persecution of the Jews living in Poland.

In 1944, even before the war ended, the Soviets started land redistribution and the nationalisation of industry in Poland. In 1947, there was electoral fraud and violence, and Boleslaw Bierut became the president. Between 1948 and 53, thousands of opponents of the communist party were eliminated. The power of the Church was curtailed in many ways. In the 1950s, new plans with a focus on heavy industry were launched. The collective farming effort failed in Poland though in other countries of Eastern Europe it was partly successful.

The story of Poland is similar to the story of Hungary, Czechoslovakia, Bulgaria, Romania and other Eastern European countries. All of them became satellite countries to the USSR and lost their freedom.

## *Korean War*

The Korean War took place between 1950 and 53, during the last years of Stalin. After Japan was defeated in the Second World War, Korea was divided between the Americans and the Soviets. The border between North Korea and South Korea was established at the 38$^{th}$ parallel.

In June 1950, North Korea attacked South Korea without any provocation. Why did it attack? The US secretary at that time mentioned certain countries that the US would defend and South Korea was not included in the list. North Korea thought that it could invade and occupy South Korea and Korean unification could take place under its leadership.

But the UN Security Council prescribed collective action against North Korea. The Security Council could do this because at that time the USSR was boycotting the Security Council over the UN's refusal to accept communist China as a member. The US did not let the UN give membership to communist China though it gave it to Taiwan. The UN forces to counter North Korea consisted of 50% US troops and 40% South Korean troops. Essentially it was a US mission. Communist North Korea was expected to have the support of China and the USSR. This was a major confrontation between US and USSR and was happening after the development of nuclear bombs.

General Douglas MacArthur successfully undid the North Korean invasion, but moving further he reached closer to China. The Chinese rushed 200,000 troops and pushed the UN forces back. Fighting China was not American president Truman's decision but the general's decision. The general thought that he should fight China and should even make use of the nuclear bomb if needed. Truman however refused it. It was Truman who had used the bomb against Japan, he was the first person and last person to use an atomic bomb. In April 1951, Truman dismissed MacArthur. By June 1953, a ceasefire was signed. Around 54,000 US soldiers died in this war. By the end of the war, Eisenhower was the new president of the US.

## *Khrushchev comes to power*

Nikita Khrushchev ruled the USSR between 1953 and 1964. However, Khrushchev was never as powerful as Stalin. The central committee of the USSR decided not to concentrate power in one person and opted for collective decision-making. After Stalin, no Soviet president came close to him in terms of accumulation of power.

During the 20$^{th}$ Soviet Party Congress held in February 1956, Khrushchev denounced Stalin. That was supposed to be a secret speech, but the whole world got to know about it. Khrushchev said that many people were killed unnecessarily during Stalin's regime. He said we should move towards a better system. Till then Stalin was being treated like a semi-god, not only in the USSR but in all other communist countries. Khrushchev's denunciation of Stalin shocked the people of many countries, including China.

Khrushchev also thought of making certain systemic changes in the USSR. He said some freedom of expression should be allowed. He said that people's consumption levels should be increased. He wanted what was called 'goulash communism', which had the aim of putting meat on every table. In Stalin's brand of communism, the focus was on heavy industry and on building the infrastructure. The economy was not devoted to the production of goods and services that would be immediately consumed, because of which the standards of living in the USSR were very low. Khrushchev wanted to change that situation, he wanted more consumption of goods and services.

Khrushchev genuinely believed in Marxism and Leninism, his objection was only to Stalin. Khrushchev did not think that the USSR was an inefficient economic or political system. In 1961, he said that the GDP of the USSR would surpass that of the US by 1980. It shows that Khrushchev was a devoted communist. Some of his reforms included abolishing the college entrance exam, making the state more lower-class oriented, and making it mandatory for students to have experience on the factory floor. During Stalin's regime, half of all the churches in the USSR were closed, and during Khrushchev's rule, half of the remaining churches were closed. In agriculture, Khrushchev promoted research on the use of new strains of hybrid corn on uncultivated lands. He also tried decentralisation of economic decision-making.

After Stalin's death, Khrushchev played politics to come to power. But once in power, he did not kill anybody. He kept his enemies at bay but did not kill them.

## *Hungarian revolution, 1956*

Khrushchev's denunciation of Stalin gave hope to some East European countries. They also thought that maybe the time has come for certain changes. Hungary was ruled since 1949 by Stalin's puppets. It went through collectivisation of agriculture and heavy industry development. There was much public resentment against the government. In 1956, there were massive protests, including student protests, and the secret police even fired at the students. The army did not side with the government.

Imre Nagy, an anti-Stalinist, came to power at this time. In Poland also, an anti-Stalinist could come to power because of the people's protests, which was not opposed by Khrushchev. After Nagy came to power, he requested the removal of the Soviet armed forces from Hungary. Nagy withdrew Hungary from the Warsaw Pact and appealed to the UN for help. In effect, he was declaring a rebellion against the USSR.

The USSR then invaded Hungary with 150,000 troops and 2,500 tanks. Thousands were killed. Nagy was hanged. Then came the Janos Kadar regime which could make some changes towards being a capitalist economy.

## *Cuban Missile Crisis*

The Cuban Missile Crisis was a situation that brought the world to the brink of a nuclear war. Those tense few days in 1962 are considered the most dangerous days humanity had ever faced.

In October 1962, the US found that the USSR kept some nuclear missiles in Cuba. The US had thought the USSR was not in a position to attack it with nuclear weapons from any of the Warsaw Pact countries, because their missiles did not have that range. The US thought it was safe. But the missiles of the US itself were kept very close to the USSR in Turkey and other places, and also the range of the US missiles was much longer.

In 1959, Fidel Castro overthrew US-backed Fulgencio Batista. Cuba came out of the US influence. The US banned sugar imports from Cuba. Castro nationalised the US firms in Cuba. Castro took the side of the USSR. The USSR promised to buy half of the sugar. Cuba quickly moved away from the US sphere of influence to the USSR sphere of influence. Castro was a committed communist.

The US did not want to have a communist country so close to its shore. Eisenhower ordered the CIA to overthrow the Castro regime. The CIA used to do such operations without any approval of Congress, it would do such things as per the president's instructions. The actual coup attempt took place in April 1961, by the time J F Kennedy became the president. That coup attempt turned out to be a fiasco.

After this, the USSR secretly placed some missiles in Cuba. The US was not supposed to know about them. And when the US got to know about it, Kennedy announced that placing the missiles in Cuba was unacceptable and Khrushchev was asked to remove them.

What would Kennedy do if Khrushchev did not remove them? Would Kennedy strike Cuba? If the US struck Cuba, there might be retaliation from the USSR, which would lead to a nuclear clash. These were very serious threats. The US though did not attack Cuba, Kennedy chose a naval blockade of Cuba instead of an airstrike. Would the USSR try to breach this blockade, and would this result in a war? That was another question. The Soviet ships on their way to Cuba went back. Finally, an agreement was reached between the superpowers. It was publicly announced that the US would never attack Cuba. The US also secretly agreed to remove its missiles in Turkey.

Khrushchev and Kennedy managed to avert the dreaded nuclear exchange. But the Soviets thought that it was Khrushchev who was responsible for bringing about this crisis. And then his retreat was considered shameful. Apart from some domestic developments, the way the Cuban Missile Crisis was handled led to Khrushchev being forced into retirement in 1964.

## *Prague Spring, 1968*

A similar thing to what happened in Hungary in 1956 happened in 1968 in Czechoslovakia, during Brezhnev's time. Brezhnev ruled the USSR from 1964 to 1982. In Czechoslovakia, Alexander Dubcek promised reforms, forcing out a Stalinist leader. He wanted a decentralised economy, relaxation of censorship, and some role for other political parties though they might be very subordinate to the communist party. He called it "socialism with a human face." These changes were known as the Prague Spring. Unlike Nagy in 1956, Dubcek said he would remain within the Soviet block. He was not questioning the Warsaw Pact, he was only calling for more moderate socialism.

But Brezhnev would not have anything of this. His concern was that one thing could lead to another. Half a million Soviet troops marched into Prague. Dubcek was taken to Moscow and was forced to make concessions. He was replaced in 1969. Prague in 1968 was less bloody than Budapest in 1956. The people here thought there was no point in resisting the USSR, so few people died unlike in Hungary over a decade earlier.

What do these things suggest? Any changes in the countries of the USSR other than Russia or the satellite countries would invite the Soviet tanks. The US or NATO would not come to defend these countries. Coming to their aid could be an invitation to World War III.

## *Think on it*

1. When were the Yalta and Potsdam conferences held? What was the outcome?
2. How did the US deal with the countries of Western Europe after the Second World War?
3. What is meant by the Sovietisation of Eastern Europe?
4. How was Germany divided after WW II?
5. What caused the Korean war? What was its outcome?
6. When was Stalin denounced by Khrushchev?
7. What were the developments in Poland in 1956?
8. What happened during the Prague Spring?
9. What is the Cuban Missile Crisis?

CHAPTER THIRTEEN

# The End of the Cold War

By 1964, Khrushchev was out and Brezhnev was in. Leonid Brezhnev became the new general secretary of the Communist Party and was the top leader in the USSR till 1982. The Brezhnev era was a long one and was marked by economic stagnation. Brezhnev said that there was terror in Stalin's period and in Khrushchev's period there was too much change and instability. Brezhnev was not known to experiment with anything. But when the system is decaying and you don't innovate, what happens? Things only get worse.

By 1987, the USSR had only 100,000 computers compared to 5 million sold annually in the US. This indicates a huge decline in science and technology and innovation. In the 50s and 60s, the USSR competed with the US in the space race, but now it was nowhere near. This was a post-industrial world, an economy dominated by services, and the Cold War superpower USSR was lagging. It had been an industrial powerhouse, but now it was failing to innovate and move ahead with the changing times.

During Brezhnev's term, the USSR was involved in many international conflicts. Brezhnev took it upon himself to fight capitalism. The arms race moved to a higher level, the Cold war was getting more intense. The USSR was trying to play a larger international role while the domestic economy was doing very poorly. In 1979, the USSR invaded Afghanistan, another proxy war with the US ensued and it started bleeding the USSR's economy.

By 1982, the political and economic situation of the USSR was very bad. After Brezhnev, two old people came to power one after another. And then came Mikhail Gorbachev who brought in drastic reforms ruled between 1985 and 1991. By the end of his term, the USSR collapsed.

## *Gorbachev*

Gorbachev

Gorbachev understood the problems of the USSR, but in trying to solve them he caused the system to crash. For quite some time, many party people came to think that the system was not delivering. The important thing was the leadership position should go to a person who understood the problem and who would change the system. Gorbachev got that opportunity.

Gorbachev introduced a policy of glasnost, which means openness. People started speaking openly, criticising Stalin and other previous regimes, and speaking against communism. There were lively debates. Gorbachev also introduced perestroika, which meant restructuring – restructuring the economy as well as the political system. The economic restructuring included reduction of subsidies, privatisation of some production and the returning of 40% of agriculture in collectivisation to individuals. Small private plots had been permitted even earlier, and they had been doing much better than the collective farms. Now there were many more of these private farms.

Gorbachev introduced these reforms at a time when the economy was at a very low point because of the Afghan crisis and the arms race. The arms race intensified during Reagan's time. Reagan even started a project called 'Star Wars' – a missile defence for the entire United States against potential nuclear attacks. The USSR was spending more and more on its military during Brezhnev's time and even after that. But it was fighting a losing battle. In 1986, a nuclear accident at Chernobyl exposed the dysfunction of the system. The damage was extensive, they couldn't contain it fast.

Gorbachev initiated many reforms after 1988. He brought in direct elections that were never there before. In the Congress of People's Deputies,1500 out of its 2250 members would now be directly elected. The Supreme Soviet or the parliament now held elections and its debates were televised live. The monopoly of the communist party came to an end.

The whole society of Soviet Russia was finally changing because of Gorbachev. He was a man with a vision. He rose to this position from humble beginnings. He was the son of a peasant and was brought up in a good family. His maternal grandfather was a member of the communist party and helped form their village's first kolkhoz or collective farm in 1929. During WW2, Gorbachev's village was invaded by the German army, but it was won back by the Soviets, so the kid was narrowly saved. The young Gorbachev knew that the collective farms were not working well. He went to study at the Moscow University where there was relatively more openness. He was bright, intelligent, hard-working, and more importantly, honest, because of which he was promoted to higher ranks in the party.

Many books that looked at communism critically which were not available to the general public were available to the communist leaders because the leaders were supposed to know about the criticism of communism. The difference between Gorbachev and other leaders was that Gorbachev read those books. He was also influenced by European communists and their views on Marxism and Leninism. He was aware of the ideas that inspired the 1968 Prague Spring and similar events. He was recognised by some powerful people within the communist party who felt that he might change things for the better.

## *1989 revolutions*

Eastern Europe

When some East European countries wanted to move away from communism during Khrushchev's reign, the USSR sent its army to crush the rebellions. Brezhnev did the same. Gorbachev explicitly said that he wouldn't interfere. Gorbachev wanted to encourage reforms in those countries as well.

Five countries in Eastern Europe – Poland, Czechoslovakia, Hungary, Romania, and Bulgaria – were under the influence of

Soviet Russia and were considered its satellites. Though Yugoslavia was an Eastern European country, socialism developed independently there.

In Poland, things had been changing from much earlier on. We can say the road to 1989 was a long one in Poland. Solidarity, a trade union, became a powerful organisation in the country in the late 70s. Nearly 1/3rd of the population joined Solidarity. Its leader was Lech Walesa. In 1981, martial law was imposed in the country and the leaders of Solidarity were jailed. But in 1988, Solidarity was restored. In September 1989, for the first time, a non-communist leader came to power. It took nearly 10 years of struggle to get one non-communist leader elected to the top position.

Hungary had been following an economic policy that was not dictated by the Soviets since 1968. It held elections in 1985, though only communists could take part in it. In 1989, Hungary gave free passage to the East Germans crossing to Austria, something which it didn't do before.

In November 1989, East Germany decided to allow its citizens free passage to West Germany. This started a mass movement of people crossing the Berlin Wall, and very soon the Wall itself was pulled down. In October 1990, East and West Germanies reunited. Helmut Kohl was the German chancellor at that time and George Bush the US president. Gorbachev allowed German unification with the assurance that NATO would not be expanded further east. He also got financial help from Germany.

In Czechoslovakia, protests against the government began in 1989. The government resigned in December that year. There was no violence. Vaclav Havel became the first post-communist president of the Czech Republic in 1990. Similarly, new governments came to power in Bulgaria and Romania.

The entire Eastern block, one country after another, moved away from communism. The struggle had been longer in Poland, and by the time the reforms came to Czechoslovakia the change was quick.

## *Collapse of USSR*

The developments in Eastern Europe were leading to independence demands within the republics of the USSR. These demands started in Estonia, Latvia and Lithuania. These three Baltic republics had been independent between 1918 and 1940 before Stalin seized them.

In 1990, Gorbachev ordered a crackdown in Lithuania when it declared its independence. He could allow East European countries to move away, but he was trying not to let the Soviet Union fall apart. Some other Soviet republics wanted to be independent. Then Gorbachev thought of restructuring the USSR into a Union of Soviet Sovereign Republics with a more decentralised structure.

The survival of the USSR was at stake. In August 1991, some communist party hardliners staged a coup to overthrow Gorbachev. He was in a retreat house then and was house-arrested there. He was asked to resign, but he did not. The coup leaders announced that Gorbachev was sick and that they were taking over the country.

But this move by some members of the Communist Party was not successful. There was no support from the people and only partial support from the army. Boris Yeltsin, the elected head of the Russian republic defied the coup. Many people gathered in Moscow to protest the coup. Gorbachev was released very soon and the coup failed.

But Yeltsin became more popular during the coup. It seemed like Yeltsin saved Gorbachev. As some republics were seeking independence, Yeltsin knit a new entity called the Commonwealth of Independent States (CIS), with 11 out of the 15 Soviet states opting to join it. The three Baltic republics and Ukraine refused to join it. When the CIS formed, the USSR was no more there and so Gorbachev could no longer be its leader. Yeltsin played a role in restoring Gorbachev, but he also played a role in the collapse of the USSR. If not for Yeltsin, a different kind of USSR might have been possible. If the biggest republic was not keen on keeping the union, how would the union survive? Gorbachev thinks Yeltsin did it because he wanted to remove Gorbachev from power.

## *Yeltsin's Russia*

Yeltsin was the president of Russia between 1991 and 1999. During the Gorbachev era, Yeltsin belonged to the radical side. Gorbachev was pulled in two different directions by radicals and conservatives. Yeltsin was a radical who wanted faster reforms. By 1991, Yeltsin was getting more popular and Gorbachev was losing popularity. All the economic turmoil Russia was going through was blamed on Gorbachev. Gorbachev was still a member of the communist party and was trying to preserve some of the old structures, whereas Yeltsin resigned from the party and was critical of it.

As Yeltsin attempted to make an abrupt transition to a market economy, many wrong things took place. There was gross mismanagement of privatisation. Massive public sector assets were sold off to individuals at very low prices. This created powerful oligarchs. Yeltsin also waged a disastrous war with Muslim Chechens.

In 1999, Putin became the Russian leader and he is still in power now more than two decades later. Russia moved towards authoritarian rule under Putin. And Eastern Europe transitioned more successfully towards democracy compared to former republics of the USSR. The damage that communism wreaked on these societies is long-lasting.

## *Think on it*

1. Why was USSR in serious trouble by the 1980s?
2. What factors led to the revolutionary changes in 1989 in the East European countries?
3. Explain the events that led to the German unification.
4. Trace the events that led to the collapse of the USSR.
5. Why is democracy difficult in Russia?

CHAPTER FOURTEEN

# The Islamic World

In the second half of the twentieth century, there was an ideological conflict between US and USSR, it was a fight between capitalism and democracy on one side and communism as Russia practised it on the other side. Towards the end of the twentieth century, the communist bloc was defeated, and the ideology of capitalism proved superior to that of communism. Both these ideologies are secular ideologies, there was no religion involved.

The battle between capitalism and communism was the defining ideological conflict of the modern era, but what was the major ideological conflict before that? One can say that it was the conflict between Islam and the modern world. The modern world started from the times of the Renaissance in Europe in the 16$^{th}$ century. Its ideology included democracy, secularism and rationality. In time these ideas spread across the whole world.

Islam started rising as a world power in the 7$^{th}$ century CE and had been a predominant influence on world affairs till almost 1700 CE. So one can say Islam had tremendous power as a source of ideology for nearly a thousand years, and even after that continued to be a strong ideology in a large part of the world.

Until the 16$^{th}$ century, there was a stand-off between Europe and the great Muslim empires. Then Renaissance and Scientific Revolution altered the balance in favour of Europe. Earlier, during the time of the crusades, the ideological battle was between Islam and Christianity, but as modernisation took over Europe, it was not a battle between Christianity and Islam anymore, it was the modern world vs Islam. By the $17^{th}$ century, there remained three Muslim empires in the world: the Mughals in India, the Ottoman Turks and the Safavid Persians who were ruling modern-day Iran. They were all overthrown or significantly weakened by the $19^{th}$ century.

Islam is based on the religious ideology developed by Prophet Mohammed in the $7^{th}$ century CE. Its major tenets include the notion that there is one God, Allah, and that Prophet Mohammed is the last messenger of Allah. The Muslims believe that the purpose of human existence is to follow and spread God's message as revealed in the Holy Quran. They believe that if you are creating a social system based on the Quran, then God himself will help you. They believe that Allah helped Prophet Mohammed in his military conquests.

In Islam, politics, religion, and military conquest all got mixed up more than in any other religion. As the Muslims went about conquering the world, they had a strong conviction that God was on their side. They had a strong social code, known as Sharia, they had a strong sense of community, and immense zeal to spread God's word by waging holy wars against infidels. Armed with that conviction, they pursued military technology, developed warfare techniques and went about establishing the Islamic rule in many countries of Asia and even Europe.

But in the end, the Islamic ideology could not survive the onslaught of modernisation. Because ultimately, whatever be your ideological convictions, it is the strength of your political and economic organisation and the impact of your military power that matter. Science and technology brought great new strength to Europe, while Islam lagged. The colonial or European powers advanced with their military might, and the Islamic empires crumbled. In India too, the British conquered the Mughals, along with other Muslim and Hindu kingdoms, and took control over the country.

## *Response to loss of power*

How the Islamic world responds to this loss of power is shaping the current political scenario. Today the Islamic world continues to exist and thrive, though it is not the world power that it had once been. It has been much easier for people to give up communism, but people cannot put aside Islam so easily because their religion has a much stronger and deeper hold on them.

After the breakup of the USSR, many communist and socialist countries embraced capitalism. Even Russia and China have changed much. Now nearly no one would think that the version of communism given by Lenin is the right economic and political model. Countries are forced to change when they realise that the ideology they have been following does not work, although they tend to do that with some resistance. But unlike an economic ideology such as communism, Islam is a religion and is a source of basic identity for hundreds of millions of people. The Muslims in many countries are not in a position to say, we are wrong, our God may be wrong. Religion by its very nature does not promote rational thinking.

Some Muslims think that Islam lost only because the Muslims did not follow true Islam. This thinking gave rise to some movements that reinforced Islamic fundamentalism such as the Salafis and the Wahabis.

If the Islamists are powerful enough in a country, they can make the entire state Islamic, as in Iran where a religious clergy led by a supreme leader makes the decisions. On the other hand, Turkey, a country that had been the centre of the Islamic world for centuries, underwent complete secularisation during the reign of Ataturk in the early part of the 20$^{th}$ century. Of all the Islamic countries now, Turkey seems to be much more successful economically and politically. Some Muslim countries in the Middle East went for what is known as Arab nationalism -- the emphasis there is not on Islam.

Still, Islam is not something like communism that could be easily swept away. Even if the political and social structure in Islamic countries changes, it is not that easy for the people to change. For example, at present Turkey is showing some signs of reverting to

Islam. The countries that followed Arab nationalism too couldn't move away from Islam. Sometimes there is a conflict between the rulers and the people. This leads to problems of adjustments, the kind of problems that socialist countries did not face earlier when they changed to capitalism or democracy.

## *Middle East*

The Muslim population of the world is currently around 1.5 billion. They continue to play a central role in the Middle East. Many countries in this region formed as a result of the breakup of the Ottoman Empire, which was one of the three Muslim empires that ruled the world for hundreds of years. It collapsed after World War I.

The central part of the Ottoman Empire was Turkey. Turkey emerged as an independent country soon after World War I. The other newly formed countries became what were called mandates to the European powers that were victorious in World War I. They would become independent nations later. A mandate is just another name for a colony. Syria and Lebanon came under the French mandate. Iraq, Palestine, and the region known as Transjordan came under the British mandate. The countries in the Arabian peninsula went through many changes in their borders before the present-day nations were formed.

This kind of colonisation created a new conflict between the West and Islam. When Palestine came under the British mandate, Britain agreed to support "a national home for the Jewish people" in Palestine while also assuring that "nothing shall be done which may prejudice the civil and religious rights of existing non-Jewish communities." This was called the Balfour Declaration and laid the groundwork for the formation of the state of Israel. The Arabs were living in that region and had been the majority there for nearly 1800 years since the Jews migrated away from their homeland.

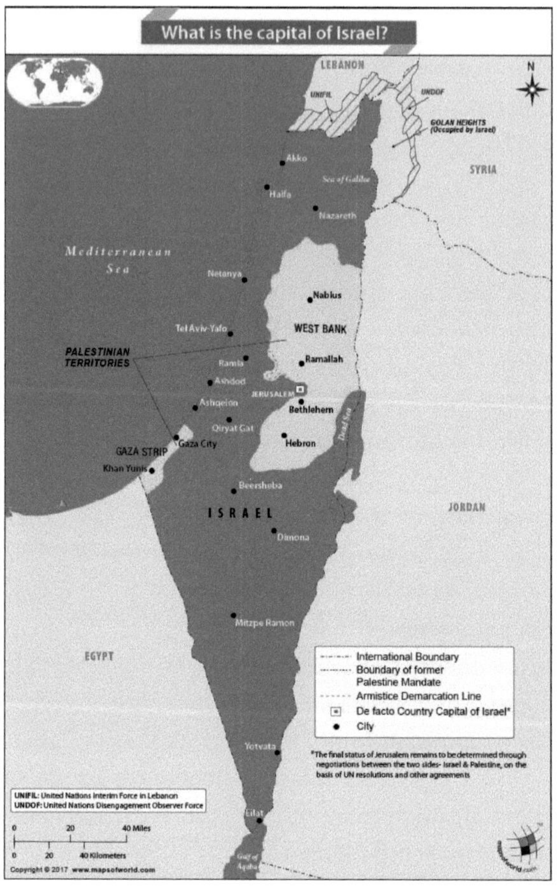


Israel

Jewish immigration from Europe and America began in the 1880s. After the Balfour Declaration, many more Jewish people came back to what they considered their home. At the outbreak of WW 2, 30% of Palestine's inhabitants were Jews. After the war, more and more Jews from different parts of the world poured into Palestine and the free nation of Israel was created in 1948. Israel was created from Palestine against the will of the Muslims. A large number of Muslims living in that region for centuries were displaced. Soon after its formation, the new state of Israel was thus pitted against its Muslim neighbours. The Palestinian Liberation Organisation (PLO) was created in 1964 to establish a Palestinian state. Israel was heavily supported by the West, and the Israel issue became a major issue between the West and the Muslim world.

Further, it so happened that vast reserves of oil were discovered in these Islamic countries of the Middle East. This complicated the equation. If the Middle East did not have oil, probably there would not have been such an intense conflict between the West and Islam. The West wanted to have control over this oil-rich region. The West was supporting dictatorships against the people in the Middle East, which led to a widely prevalent anti-West sentiment there. It was resentment against the political and economic domination of the West. And because these people had a strong identity with their religion, this conflict became a conflict of the Muslims vs the West.

Islam became a kind of the connecting point, a way to organise resistance against the actual or perceived Western domination. Some people think that even if there had been no Islamic factor, the things that the US and European countries did in the Middle East would still have generated an anti-West sentiment there. Islam further exacerbated the anti-West sentiment.

## *Nature of Islam*

Islam is different from other religions in some important respects. Islam is more comprehensive in its scope than Christianity and other religions, it is a religion that seeks to cover most aspects of life and society. It seeks to shape and influence politics, economics, and social norms, along with the belief systems related to god, heaven, hell and spirituality. In most cases, religion has something to do with worship, rituals, belief systems related to the soul and afterlife, some kind of spirituality and moral code, but it may not go beyond that. Buddha left his kingdom taking no interest in politics, Jesus had no interest in politics, but Mohammed was a warrior, a politician, and a ruler. He gave moral code in all aspects of life.

Besides adhering to the form of worship and belief system prescribed by the Quran, a true Muslim is expected to be a part of the appropriate political and economic system. To a vast number of Christians, at least in our times, their religion is only about going to the church on Sundays, but Islam is rarely confined to the practice of going to the mosque every Friday. A great number of Muslims tend to be more serious about their religion. Their faith impinges on many aspects of life.

Also, Islam promotes a stronger sense of community compared to other religions. All the Muslims of the world from various countries tend to feel connected. A great example of this is the Khilafat movement during the early days of India's freedom struggle when so many Indian Muslims wanted to take part in the defence of the Ottoman Empire in the aftermath of World War I. There has always been a widespread sense of community among the Muslims of the world, and it is present even now. In recent years we can see an example of this in the growing reach of the distinctly terrorist organisation of Islamic State, with Muslims from various countries, including those in the West, showing the willingness to sacrifice their lives for their religion by joining this organisation.

The extent of secularisation that happened in various other religions of the world such as Christianity did not happen in Islam. From a historical perspective, the problem with Islam currently is that it may be impacting how people are responding to political issues. Again going back to India's freedom struggle, there was a conflict between British imperialism and India, but how did India deal with it? The leaders of the freedom movement did not give a call on the Hindus to be true Hindus, rather they strove to educate the people and modernise the country. In many cases, the Islamic religion may be preventing a modern response to modern problems. Instead of trying to adapt to a new situation, the Muslims in many countries tend to take recourse to Islam to solve their problems.

During the Arab Spring, people came out onto the streets and chucked out the dictators. It looked like this could bring about a great change. But after successfully overthrowing the dictatorial regimes, the people couldn't agree on what should be an alternative. The people ended up electing parties that were Islamic and authoritarian, the people did not have unity, and they did not have a consensus on a democratic and secular alternative. When their opinions were sought, the people were divided on the role of their religion, while some thought that it was the source of the problem, others thought that Islam is the solution.

In non-Islamic countries, people do not generally debate the role of their religion in politics or society, but why should Muslims do so? It is because of inadequate secularisation. While some people in the Muslim countries developed modern values, most others are lagging. It may be difficult for many Muslims even to conceive that they should make decisions on many things such as what women's rights are, what people's rights are, and what kind of a political system they want to have, without any reference to the Quran or the Prophet. It would help if the Muslims stop thinking of everything in terms of their religion, and realise how modernisation means freedom from religion and the separation of the society from the state.

Some liberal-thinking Muslims in Islamic countries are on the verge of desperation about the role of religion in society. This can be seen in a recent phenomenon in Turkey, where people developed a strange new concept of freedom to go to hell. They don't want to get into any futile debates about the existence of heaven and hell, they concede, okay, there is hell, and if we don't follow the precepts of Islam to the letter, we will go to hell, but still they insist that they should have the freedom to go to hell. People should have the freedom to make their own choices, even if that means going to hell. It's not the role of the government to prevent people from going to hell. This may look a little weird, but I think it is a good sign and this kind of new thinking is needed. The right to go to hell may be declared a fundamental right in Islamic countries.

Interestingly, although we tend to have an image of Islam as a fundamentalist religion that tends to create a theocratic state when Islam was spreading from one country to another over centuries, it did not do so as a completely intolerant religion. On the contrary, many successful Muslim rulers were tolerant and accommodating. Islam picked up many things from the societies it conquered. If you define Islam simply as the Quran plus some hadiths and you go for their literal interpretation, then it produces very rigid thinking. If you include in Islam many additional things it picked during its spread, it becomes like any other religion.

Unfortunately, people who added other things to Islam never criticised the core. For example, the Sufis did not say that Prophet Mohammed was wrong. They only said that Prophet Mohammed was the first Sufi. They interpreted the religion without criticising the core. That is why if some person comes and says, this is the core and everything else is a deviation, it creates some legitimate audience for him. This encourages fundamentalism.

## *Think on it*

1. What are the central tenets of Islam?
2. To whom did Islamic ideology lose in terms of power?
3. What are the various responses of the Muslims to the loss of power of Islam?
4. How can one explain religious fundamentalism as seen in Islam?
5. How were independent nations created out of the breakup of the Ottoman Empire?
6. What is the concept of 'mandate' in the context of the Middle East?
7. How did Israel become an issue between the West and the Islamic world?
8. What is the role of oil in creating conflict between the West and Islam?
9. How is Islam different from other world religions?
10. How is Islam responding to the problems of the modern world?
11. Why did not the Arab Spring lead to democracies?
12. How is Islam prone to encourage fundamentalism?

# Sources

1. World Civilizations Volume II: Since 1500 by Philip J Adler & Randall L. Pouwels, 7th (2015) edition

2. Twentieth-Century by Findley and Rothney, 6th (2006) edition

3. A History of Modern Europe: From The Renaissance to the Present by John Merriman, 3rd (2010) edition

4. Documentaries on YouTube from various sources

Printed by Libri Plureos GmbH in Hamburg,
Germany